modern

------

macrame

------

style

20 stylish beginner projects for the home with
step-by-steps, techniques, tips and tricks

modern
macrame
style

20 stylish beginner projects for the home with
step-by-steps, techniques, tips and tricks

AMAIA MARTIN

Photographs by Jesse Wild & Amaia Martin

WHITE OWL

Thank you to my partner Andy for always supporting me in all my creative journeys, and to my family and friends for their encouragement and for being my number one cheerleaders.

First published in Great Britain in 2022 by
PEN & SWORD WHITE OWL
An imprint of Pen & Sword Books Ltd
Yorkshire – Philadelphia

Copyright © Amaia Martin, 2022
@laterramacrame

ISBN 9781399014854

Group Publisher: Jonathan Wright
Series Editor and Publishing Consultant: Katherine Raderecht
Art Director: Jane Toft
Editor: Katherine Raderecht
Photography: Jesse Wild
Styling: Katherine Raderecht

Printed and bound in the UK, by Short Run Press Limited, Exeter.

Pen & Sword Books Ltd incorporates the Imprints of Pen & Sword Books
Pen & Sword Books Limited incorporates the imprints of Atlas, Archaeology, Aviation, Discovery, Family History, Fiction, History, Maritime, Military, Military Classics, Politics, Select, Transport, True Crime, Air World, Frontline Publishing, Leo Cooper, Remember When, Seaforth Publishing, The Praetorian Press, Wharncliffe Local History, Wharncliffe Transport, Wharncliffe True Crime and White Owl.

For a complete list of Pen & Sword titles please contact:
PEN & SWORD BOOKS LIMITED
47 Church Street, Barnsley, South Yorkshire S70 2AS, England
E-mail: enquiries@pen-and-sword.co.uk
Website: www.pen-and-sword.co.uk
or
PEN AND SWORD BOOKS
1950 Lawrence Rd, Havertown, PA 19083, USA
E-mail: Uspen-and-sword@casematepublishers.com
Website: www.penandswordbooks.com

FSC
www.fsc.org
MIX
Paper from
responsible sources
FSC® C014540

contents

introduction

I was born into a creative family. From my grandma, who used to knit my jumpers, winter hats and the cosiest socks, as well as making handmade soap for the whole family, to my mum, who has always had a passion for upcycling and interior design. In fact, I've grown up seeing both my parents renovate every home that we've ever lived in from scratch!

From a very young age I was drawn to painting and crafting. My parents encouraged my brother and I to experiment and play without worrying about us getting dirty, which allowed my imagination to run free. I remember that my favourite Christmas present was a Mould and Paint Aladdin clay set; my mum and I would spend many happy hours together making magical figurines.

After a bad life experience in 2011, I felt I needed to take back control of my life and reshape it in the way I wanted. I left my small town in the North of Spain and embarked on a journey to London that would change my life completely and expand my horizons in ways that I never thought possible.

Changing my quiet life to one full of possibilities was extremely exciting. However, life in a big city can be demanding, and after 5 years, I experienced stress as never before.

In Spain, a walk by the sea would have given my mind a rest, but in London I had to find an alternative way to destress, so I began crafting again.

Making things with my hands became a positive outlet for me when things were not going quite the way I wanted. So much so, that in 2018, at a point where I had grown weary of the corporate world, I set up La Terra Macramé, my own online business. My hope was that my creations would make people as happy as they made me.

The crafting world has always been dominated by unsustainable materials resistant to biodegradation, such as acrylic and synthetic fibres, polymer clay, plastic beads and glitter. I didn't want my small business to have a negative impact on the environment, so I researched sustainable alternatives. I found I could use raw, natural and recycled fibres that not only add character and texture to my creations but are also kind to our planet.

After discovering macramé and the benefits it had on my mental health, I wanted to share my knowledge and teach workshops in London. Now, I am sharing a selection of my favourite knots and projects with you in this book.

The best way to use this book is to pick the project that appeals to you most; find a calm, comfortable space at home free from distractions; play some relaxing music; light your favourite scented candles; make a cup of tea or coffee and start knotting away!

I hope that these pages bring you some peace.
Happy knotting!
Amaia

the basics

Macramé can seem a difficult craft to master at first but there is nothing to worry about. I've met many people who don't consider themselves at all "crafty" but all of them have managed at some level to create a piece of their own. That's the beauty of arts and crafts; you learn to make something with your own hands and, regardless of the result, it is a part of you and your creative journey. The most important thing is that you enjoy every single moment of the crafting experience.

I find macramé extremely therapeutic. It helps me be present and frees my mind as knotting is a sequence of rhythmic movements that feel almost like a dance.

Not all the projects in this book require the same set up. For some projects you might want to work on a flat, horizontal surface. For others, a vertical set up using hooks or dowels, or even standing up will work better. You will quickly find what suits you best. Make the most of your macramé time by creating a serene space for creation with some light music, scented candles and preferably no distractions. I hope this book helps you catch the macramé bug.

TOOLS AND APPLIANCES

The most important tools you will need to make macramé are your hands, some rope, and some scissors. However, having the following tools to hand will make creating your projects easier:

1. Wooden or metal hoops
2. Wooden or metal dowels
3. S-shaped hooks
4. Tape measure
5. Washi tape
6. Clothes rack
7. Macramé wooden slicker brush

Before starting a project, I suggest that you first read the instructions in full, making sure that you have all the tools and materials required. You will also want everything prepared and within reach so you don't have to stop your crafting unexpectedly.

MATERIALS

The craft and decoration industry is filled with products made of plastic, polymer clays and synthetic materials. Sadly, none of these are biodegradable or recyclable and, as a result, they are harmful to our planet.

When I created my business, La Terra Macramé, one thing was very clear to me - sustainability would be at the core of my business and I would always use raw and natural materials where ever possible.

This promise has allowed me to discover a range of new fibres and experiment with different textures. This is not only fun but also adds a dramatic effect to some of my projects!

In this book, you will work with a variety of recycled materials including cotton rope, jute, raffia, recycled sari silk and linen amongst others.

If neutral colours are not your thing and you are after a more eclectic look, recycled cotton rope is extremely easy to dye naturally by using avocado, purple cabbage, beets, spinach, turmeric or even onion peels.

These are the main ropes that you will be using for your projects:
■ 3 mm 3 ply cotton rope
■ 3 mm 1 ply cotton rope
■ 5 mm 3 ply cotton rope
■ 5 mm 1 ply cotton rope
■ 5 mm braided cotton rope
■ 14 mm 3 ply cotton rope
■ 2 mm jute rope
■ 6 mm jute rope
■ Raffia
■ Velvet ribbon
■ Cotton frizz ribbon
■ Flax linen frizz ribbon
■ Recycled sari silk ribbon

If you need advice on where to find tools, appliances, and materials, I have created a go-to list of suppliers. Head to page 111.

estimating lengths

Macramé is such a beautiful art. You can use the knots to create an infinite number of patterns and shapes. What I like most is that however many you create, no two patterns will turn out the same. That is the beauty of handmade products - to embrace the imperfections!

There is no worse feeling than running out of rope midway through your project - or even worse, almost at the end.
To make sure this doesn't happen, I have given the correct measures of rope for each project in this book. However, once you learn some of the knots, you might want to start exploring, designing your own pieces or even making alterations to one of the book's patterns. When you start experimenting with macramé yourself you will need to estimate the amount of rope you will need. Unfortunately, there is no exact way of doing this. There are certain aspects of the design that will make the amount you need variable, including the thickness of the cord you use, the design, the patterns you want to create, how heavily knotted they are, and lastly, the overall size of the piece.

There is, however, a golden rule in macramé that I use to estimate the length of rope that I need for a project. Even if it is still just an estimate, it has helped me so far. Firstly, I sketch the piece that I am going to make and then divide it into sections depending on the different patterns. For

example, I will sketch a wall hanging that will start with a set of alternating square knots measuring 10 cm in height, followed by 10 cm of diamonds, another 10 cm of alternating square knots and a 30 cm long fringe. This will give me a total of 4 sections.
If the section of the pattern that I am creating is tight and the knots are knotted together, or less than 2 cm apart, I multiply the length of that section by 8.
If the area of the pattern that I am creating is looser, and the knots are knotted more than 2 cm apart, I multiply the length of that area by 6.
If I want to add some fringe at the end, I multiply the length of the fringe by 2.
Add the length of each part of your project together and add 10% to get your final rope measurement.

So, returning to the example above, I would make the following calculation:
10 cm x 8 = 80 cm
10 cm x 8 = 80 cm
10 cm x 8 = 80 cm
30 cm x 2 = 60 cm
Total = 300 cm + 10% = 330 cm

I would therefore need 3.30 m long cords to create this pattern.
Don't worry if you have excess rope after a project, you can always use these trimmings to add tassels, or fringes to other projects.
If you are using a thick rope, over 6 mm for example, I would add 20% instead of 10% to the final measurement to be on the safe side.

knots & techniques

Even though the origins of macramé are not known, what is clear is that macramé knots have been used for centuries to create garments, soft furnishings and hangings. The knots that you are about to learn will give you the tools to make hundreds of designs, from more classic pieces to contemporary creations. Whatever your decorative style, there is a macramé knot for you. The following knots are perfect for both complete beginners and crafters who want to get back into macramé again!

LARK'S HEAD KNOT

A lark's head knot is the most common knot to start a piece of macramé. When you add rope onto a dowel, ring or another piece of rope, this is the knot that you tend to use.

1. Fold the cord in half making a loop on the top of the cord. Place this loop on top of the dowel/cord. **(Fig. 1.)**

2. Pass the loop over and behind the dowel/cord. **(Fig. 2.)**

3. Thread the ends of the cord through the loop. **(Fig. 3.)**

4. Pull the cords down until firmly tighten making sure that the ends meet.

REVERSE LARK'S HEAD KNOT

1. Fold the cord in half, making a loop on the top of the cord. Place this loop behind the dowel/cord. **(Fig. 1.)**

2. Fold the loop over and in front of the dowel/cord. **(Fig. 2.)**

3. Thread the ends of the cord through the loop. **(Fig. 3.)**

4. Pull the cords down until firmly tighten making sure that the ends meet. **(Fig. 4.)**

DIAGONAL HALF HITCH KNOT

This double half hitch knot is ideal to create patterns like diamonds and add movement to a piece. You will use an anchor cord onto which all the knots will be attached. You will make 2 double half hitch knots with each working cord.

LEFT DIAGONAL DOUBLE HALF HITCH

 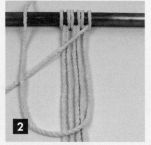 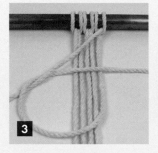 

1. Take the far right cord 6 (anchor) and hold it over the working cords at a diagonal angle. **(Fig. 1.)**

2. Pass the next cord in line, cord number 5, behind the anchor cord and create a U-shape that goes over the diagonal anchor. **(Fig. 2.)**

3. Once cord number 5 is over the anchor, thread it through the centre of the U-shape. **(Fig. 3.)**

4. Pull the knot up tightly and repeat these steps using the same cord before moving to the next cord in line, cord number 4. **(Fig. 4.)**

RIGHT DIAGONAL DOUBLE HALF HITCH

 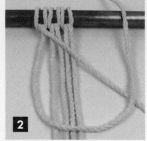  

1. Take the far left cord 1 (anchor) and hold it over the working cords in a diagonal angle. **(Fig. 1.)**

2. Pass the next cord in line, cord number 2, behind the anchor cord and create a U- shape that goes over the diagonal anchor. **(Fig. 2.)**

3. Once cord number 2 is over the anchor, thread it through the centre of the U-shape. **(Fig. 3.)**

4. Pull the knot up tightly and repeat these steps using the same cord before moving to the next cord in line, cord number 3. **(Fig. 4.)**

DIAMOND PATTERN

Macramé diamonds are a great pattern for wall hangings and look beautiful when you work a sinnet (a series) of diamonds one on top of the other. In this example, you'll work with 4 cords that will be attached to a dowel using a lark head's knot. This will give you 8 cords to work with, 1 to 8 from left to right.

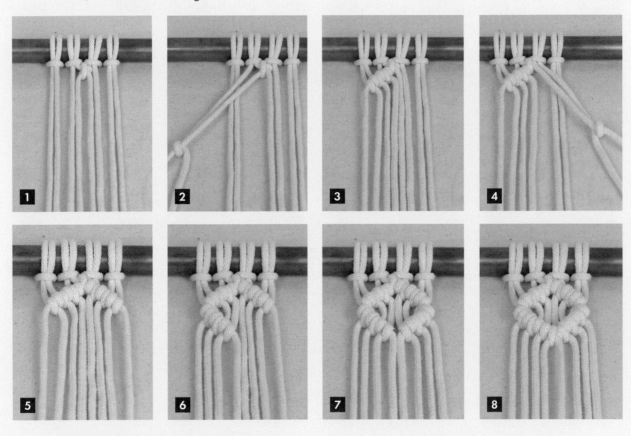

1. Start by making a double half hitch knot with cord 4 and 5. These 2 cords will be your anchor cords. **(Fig. 1.)**

2. Using cord 4, work a left diagonal double half hitch knot attaching cords 3, 2 and 1 to your anchor cord 4. **(Figs. 2. & 3.)**

3. Using cord 5, work a right diagonal double half hitch knot attaching cords 6, 7 and 8 to your anchor cord 5. This will create a little triangle shape. **(Figs. 4. & 5.)**

4. Now you are going to create the bottom half of your macramé diamond. Using cord 1 as your anchor, attach cords 2, 3 and 4 to it using a right diagonal double half hitch knot. **(Fig. 6.)**

5. Using cord 8 as your anchor, attach cords 7, 6 and 5 to it using a left diagonal double half hitch knot. **(Fig. 7.)**

6. Finish your macramé diamond by connecting the bottom half. Make a double half hitch knot to the anchor cords. **(Fig. 8.)**

HORIZONTAL DOUBLE HALF HITCH KNOT

A horizontal double half hitch knot is a great knot to learn for cushions, table runners or to add a horizontal line to a wall hanging design.

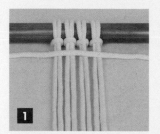

1. Cut a piece of rope that covers the length of the area of the horizontal line you want plus 4cm on each end. This cord will be your anchor.

2. Place this cord horizontally from left to right on top of all the other cords (working cords). **(Fig. 1.)**

3. To create a row of knots, you will attach the working cords to your anchor by tying double half hitch knots. **(Figs. 2. & 3.)**

4. You can leave the excess 4 cm on both sides or hide them by threading them to the back of your piece. After you have secured them, cut any excess. I recommend you use a large eyed knitting needle to help with this step. **(Fig. 4.)**

BERRY KNOT

The berry knot is one of my favourite knots to add texture or to add pattern to my design.

It is made using a combination of square knots. You will only work the outer cords (working cords 1 & 4) leaving the middle cords (filler cords 2 & 3) unused until step 2.

This knot uses more cord than other knots, so bear this in mind for any future designs.

1. Leaving a gap of ½ cm **(Fig. 1.)** make 3 consecutive square knots **(Fig. 2.)** (Page 15)

2. Take the filler cords 2 & 3 and weave them through the middle hole at the top of the first square

knot. Pull all the way through until the square knots curl upwards forming a berry shape. **(Fig. 3.)**

3. To secure the knot, tie half a square knot or a full square knot underneath the berry. **(Fig. 4.)**

SQUARE KNOT

A square knot is one of the classic and most used knots in macramé. To make this knot you will only need to work with the outer cords (working cords) 1 & 4, whilst the middle cords (filler cords) 2 & 3, will remain unused.

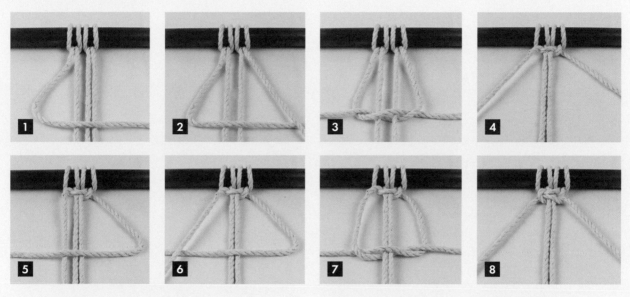

1. Make a loop in the shape of a number 4 with cord number 1, extending the tail across the filler cords and cord 4. **(Fig. 1.)**
2. Now thread cord 1 behind cord 4. **(Fig. 2.)**
3. Then run cord number 4 under the filler cords (3 and 2) and up through the back of cord number 1´s loop. **(Fig. 3.)** Pull both the left and right cords to tighten, while holding the filler cords down. See Tip below. This is a half square knot. **(Fig. 4.)**

4. Now reverse the process to complete the knot: make a loop in the shape of a P with cord 4, extending the tail across the filler cords and cord 1. **(Fig. 5.)**
5. Now thread cord 4 behind cord 1. **(Fig. 6.)**
6. Run cord 1 under the filler cords (2 and 3) and up through the back of cord number 4's loop. **(Fig. 7.)** Pull both working cords to tighten, while holding the filler cords down. Your square knot is finished! **(Fig. 8.)**

> **AMAIA'S TIP** When pulling the working cords in points number 3 and 6, the filler cords might move up into the middle of your knot. To stop this from happening, if you are working in a horizontal set up or on top of a surface, you can hold down the filler cords with washi tape or your fingers whilst pulling the working cords. If you are working in a vertical set up, you can hold the filler cords down by stepping on them if you are standing up or by clamping them between your knees if you are sitting down. This will let you to work faster.

ALTERNATING SQUARE KNOTS

An alternating square knot is a great way of forming an interconnected woven design. You can make your design looser by leaving more space between rows, less to create a tighter design or for the tightest weave possible, leave no space.

1. Create a row of as many square knots as you would like for your design. **(Fig. 1.)** (For the projects in this book, the number of knots are specified.)

2. Start an alternating pattern by making additional square knots using the 2 right hand cords from the left knot and the 2 left hand cords from the right knot. **(Fig. 2.)**

3. Alternate steps 1 and 2 to continue the pattern. **(Fig. 3.)**, **(Fig. 4.)**

SPIRAL KNOT

A spiral knot is another classic and often used knot in macramé. To make it, you will also only need to work with the outer cords (working cords) 1 & 4, whilst the middle cords (filler cords) 2 & 3, remain unused.

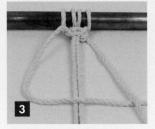
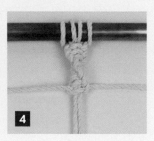

1. Make a loop in the shape of a number 4 with the cord number 1, extending the tail across cords 2, 3 and behind 4. **(Fig. 1.)**

2. Run cord number 4 under the filler cords (2 and 3) and up through the back of cord number 1's loop. **(Fig. 2.)**

3. Pull both the left and right cords to tighten, while holding the filler cords down. This is called a half square knot. **(Fig. 3.)** See Tip Page 15.

4. Now instead of reversing the process, as in the square knot, continue making half square knots as in points 1 to 3. **(Fig. 4.)** See Tip opposite.

> **AMAIA'S TIP** If the knot is not tightening evenly between both cords or you see a gap, try pulling one of the other working cords and this should correct the asymmetry. You can then pull both working cords to make sure the knot is tight.

CROWN KNOT

You can make this knot using 2, 4 or 8 cords depending how chunky you want your design to be. In this example, I use 2 cords. For 4 cords, you would start step 1 dividing the 4 cords in 2 groups of 2, or 2 groups of 4 for a total of 8 cords.

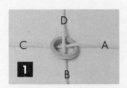

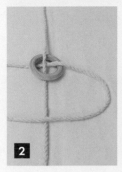 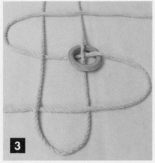 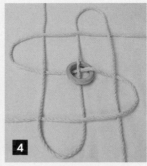  

1. Thread the first cord over and under a wooden ring and the second cord under and over the wooden ring creating a cross. **(Fig. 1.) 2.** Place the A cord on top of the B cord creating a U shape. **(Fig. 2.).**
3. Place the B cord on top of the C cord. After that, cord C will go on top of cord D respectively. **(Fig. 3.)**

4. Thread the end of the D cord through the U shape on its right (it is the first U shape you made with the A cord). **(Fig. 4.)**
5. Carefully pull the end of the A, B, C and D cords until you have tightly secured the knot. **(Fig. 5.)**
6. Repeat these steps to create the pattern **(Fig. 6.).**

GATHERING KNOT

 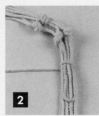    

1. Cut a piece of wrapping cord at least 1 metre long. Use the first 25 cm to fold into a U shape and lay this vertically on top of the bundle of cord. **(Fig. 1.)**
2. Starting at the top (leaving at least 3cm of cord unwrapped) begin wrapping the cord to the right encompassing all your cord. **(Fig. 2.)** Keep going round using firm but not too tight pressure. Stop wrapping when you are happy with the length of your knot or until there is only about 3 cm of the loop

exposed, whichever comes first. **(Fig. 3.).**
3. Thread the end of the wrapping cord through this loop. **(Fig. 4.)** Pull up on the cord at the top of the wrap to slide your threaded loop underneath the wrapped cord. Stop when you reach about halfway up your gathering knot. **(Fig. 5.)**
4. Trim the excess wrapping cord at both ends and use your scissor tips to push the excess cord under your gathering knot so it is nicely hidden. **(Fig. 6.)**

RYA KNOT

Who doesn't like a good tassel? The rya knot is an easy way of adding fun and movement to your macramé or weaving designs.

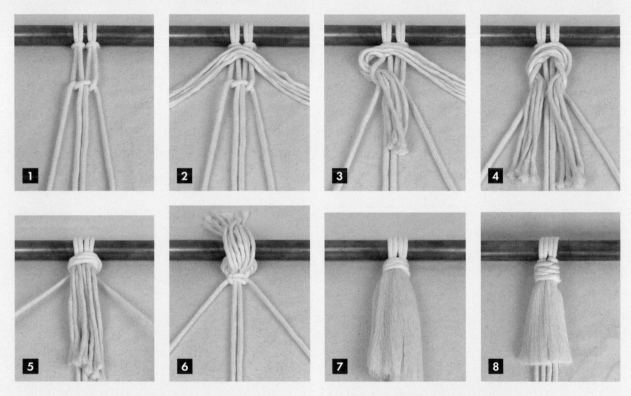

1. Cut around 6 pieces of 25 cm long cord. (The amount of cord and length will vary depending on how chunky and long you want your tassels to be).

2. Make a half square knot. **(Fig. 1.)**

3. Take the 6 pieces of cord making sure that the ends meet and fold them in half making a loop. Take the centre of this loop and put it on top of cords 2 and 3 (filler cords). **(Fig. 2.)**

4. Pass the sides of the cords around the front of cords 1 and 4 bringing the end of these cords to the front through the gap in between cord 1-2 and 3-4. Pull this group of cords slightly. **(Figs. 3. & 4.)**

5. Pull the cords 1 and 4 tightly until the tassel is formed. If you prefer to hold it more tightly in place, finish the half square knot you made in step 2 making another half square knot. **(Figs. 5. & 6.)**

6. If you have used a 1 ply cotton rope, you can now brush the bottom of the tassels. To do so, you can use a hair comb to start combing the ends and work your way up. You can also use a wooden slicker brush for a more professional finish. **(Fig. 7.)**

7. Cut the tassels to your preferred length by cutting away any excess length. **(Fig. 8.)**

RYA KNOT IN A MACRAMÉ DIAMOND

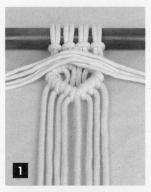

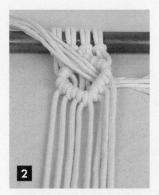

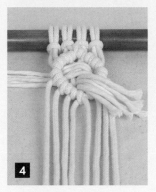

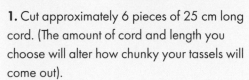

1. Cut approximately 6 pieces of 25 cm long cord. (The amount of cord and length you choose will alter how chunky your tassels will come out).

2. Take the 6 pieces of cord, making sure that the ends meet, and fold them in half making a loop to mark the halfway point. Then, take the centre point of this loop and lay it flat on top of the diamond. **(Fig. 1.)**

3. Thread the ends of the 6 cords through the gap on the right-hand side of the diamond. **(Fig. 2.)** Pull until the centre point of the cords is in the centre of the diamond.

4. Repeat Step 3 threading the end of the 6 cords through the gap on the left-hand side of the diamond. Adjust both ends until all the 6 cords are flat and centred in the diamond. **(Fig. 3.)**

5. Now thread the ends of the 6 cords from the back to the front of the diamond, starting with the right side. Thread them through the middle gap of the diamond. Pull slightly. **(Fig. 4.)**

6. Repeat Step 5 now with the left side. **(Fig. 5.)**

7. If you have used a 1 ply cotton rope, you can now brush the bottom of the tassels. Use a hair comb and comb the ends working your way up. You can also use a wooden slicker brush for a more professional finish.

8. Cut your tassels to your preferred length. **(Fig. 6.)**

chapter one: plant hangers

Being in nature helps us feel more relaxed and reduces any anxiety and stress we might be experiencing. In a big city like London, where having a garden, balcony or terrace can be difficult, having indoor plants is a great way to enjoy plants. Plant hangers will add bohemian style to your home and are a great way to create extra space for your plant collection when you run out of floor space. In this chapter, you will learn how to create a selection of plant hangers that mix different styles, materials and colours.

handmade beads plant hanger

This plant hanger is great fun to make. Not only does it use an extremely satisfying knot - the spiral knot, which resembles a DNA strand - but you also have the opportunity to make your own beads if you want to. If you decide to make the beads out of air-dry clay, you will need to make them at least 24 hours in advance so that they dry completely. Simply take a piece of air-dry clay, roll it in your hands until you create a sphere, carve some decorations into it with a little toothpick if you want to be more creative and have fun experimenting. Just don't forget to make a hole through the middle with a pencil or pen!

You will need
- 21.6 m cotton braided rope (5 mm diameter)
- 5 cm wooden ring
- Terracotta air dry clay (or any 3 shop-bought beads of your choice with a hole of at least 4 mm)
- Large eye knitting needle
- Tape measure
- Scissors
- Hook

Knots you will use
- Gathering knot (Page 17)
- Spiral knot (Page 16)

Preparation
Cut: 6 pieces of 3.60 m long and 2 pieces of 0.75 m long

AMAIA'S TIP
- Generally, when using braided rope, make sure that you use the same pressure when making each knot. This kind of rope is a bit stretchy, so it is better to make a looser knot than if you were using a 1 or 3 ply recycled cotton rope.

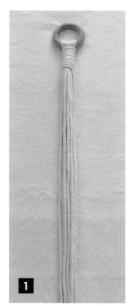

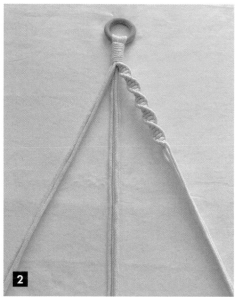

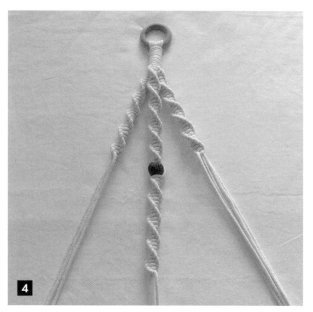

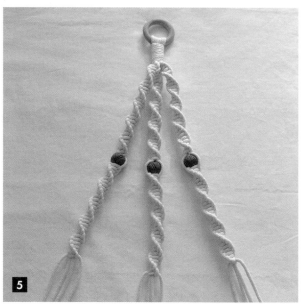

1. Start by hanging the wooden ring in a hook. Thread the 6 pieces of braided cord through the wooden ring. The easiest way to do this is by holding the end of the 6 pieces of cord and threading them through the ring together instead of one by one. There should be roughly equal lengths of cord on either side of the ring.

2. Take 1 of the smaller cotton cords and make a gathering knot of approximately 4 cm long. **(Fig. 1.)**

3. Divide the 12 pieces of cord into 3 groups of 4. Take the 1st group of 4 cords and make 30 spiral knots. **(Fig. 2.)** Repeat this with the other 2 groups.

4. Take the outer most cords and pass them between the inner cords, then thread them through the bead.

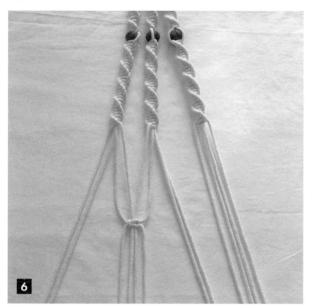

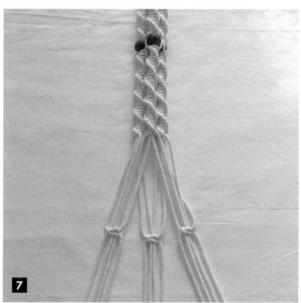

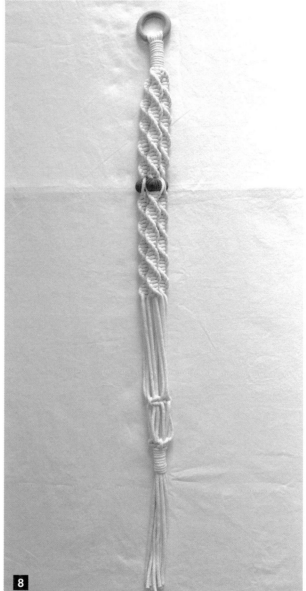

(Fig. 3.) Make 30 spiral knots. (Fig. 4.)

5. Repeat steps 4 and 5 on the other 2 groups.
(Fig. 5.)

6. Leaving an 18 cm gap, take the 2 right hand cords of any group and the 2 left hand cords of the group to the right of this one. Using these 4 cords, make 1 square knot. (Fig. 6.) Continuing to work to your right, repeat this process 2 more times so all the cords are connected. (Fig. 7.)

7. Leaving a 6 cm gap, repeat step 6.

8. Take the other small piece of cord and make a gathering knot of approximately 4 cm long. Trim the tail of the plant hanger at the length of your choice and you are finished! (Fig. 8.)

The decisive Moment/
Photographs by Henri Cartier-Bresson

26

crown knot plant hanger

Who said that macramé can't look modern? If you prefer a more contemporary look in your home, this plant hanger is perfect for you. It will still be a real statement piece due to the sinnet of crown knots at the top, however, in this plant hanger, the star of the show will always be your plant!

You will need:
- 29 m cotton braided rope (5 mm diameter)
- 5 cm wooden ring
- Tape measure
- Scissors

Knots that you will use
- Crown knot (Page 17)
- Gathering knot (Page 17)

Preparation
Cut: 8 pieces of 3.50 m long and 1 piece of 1 m long

AMAIA'S TIP
- I particularly love this hanger with any cool hanging philodendrons.
- This knot might look a bit tricky at first, however, once you start practising it you will see that there is nothing to fear.

Philodendron Micans is a tropical plant from Central America, with pretty velvety heart-shaped green leaves with reddish-purple backs.

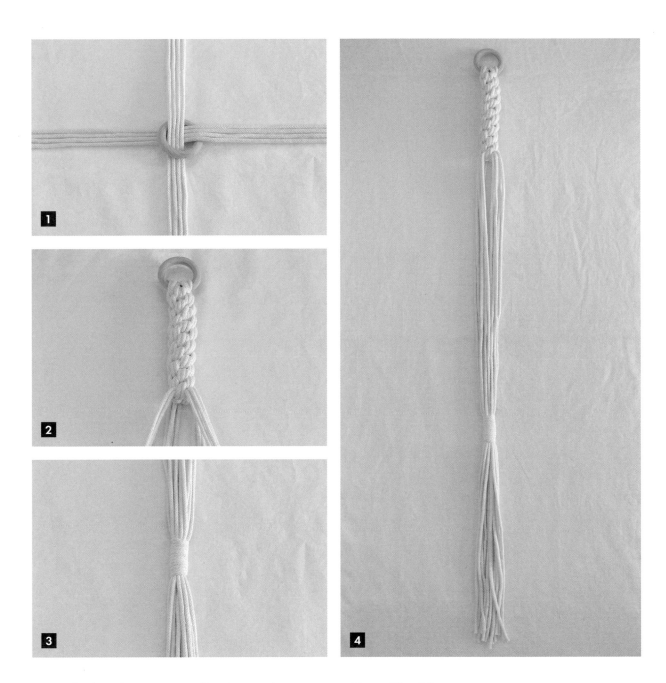

1. Start by threading 4 pieces of 3.50 m cord over and under a wooden ring and the remaining 4 cords under and over the wooden ring to create a cross. **(Fig. 1.)**

2. Now you are ready to start creating your crown knots. Work enough crown knots to create a length of 16 cm. **(Fig. 2.)**

3. Leaving a 50 cm gap, make a gathering knot of around 5 cm long using the 1 m cord (the equivalent of 12 loops). **(Fig. 3.)**

4. Cut the tail at the height of your choice. I cut mine at 35 cm. You are ready to hang you plant. **(Fig. 4.)**

jute plant hanger

Jute is one of my favourite fibres. Originally from India and obtained from the plants Corchorus olitorius and Corchorus capsularis, jute adds an incredible texture to your designs, making your creation look extremely natural and cosy. Jute doesn't absorb water as much as cotton does, so if you would like to have a plant hanger that you can hang in a porch, jute is for you!

You will need
- 24 m jute rope (6 mm diameter)
- 2 m jute rope (2 mm diameter)
- 5 cm wooden ring
- Tape measure
- Scissors
- Hook

Knots that you will use
- Gathering knot (Page 17)
- Square knot (Page 15)
- Spiral knot (Page 16)

Preparation
- Cut: 6 pieces of 4 m long of the 6 mm jute rope and 2 pieces of 1 m long of the 2 mm jute rope

AMAIA'S TIPS
- I wouldn't recommend you keep a jute hanger outside permanently, as water will penetrate the fibre at some point and over time, it might damage your beautiful creation.
- Because of the nature of this natural fibre, be careful when working with it, as it is not the softest material. Take it easy when you tighten your knots.

31

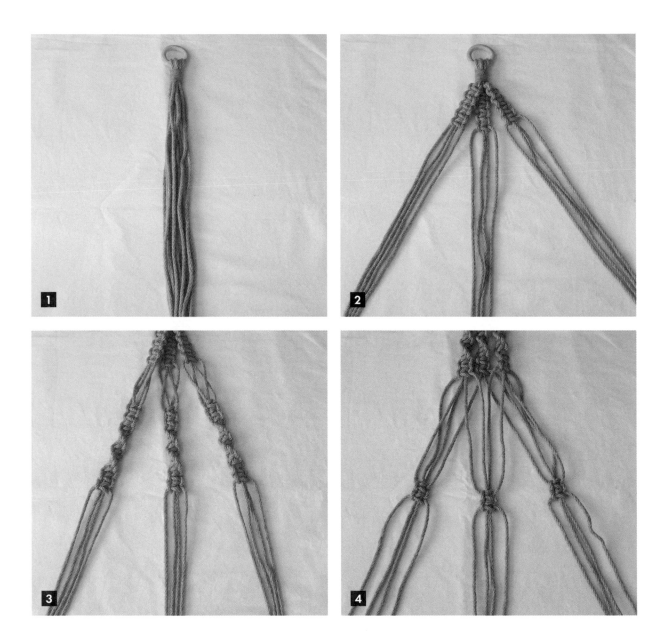

1. Hang the wooden ring in a hook. Thread the 6 pieces of jute cord through the wooden ring. The easiest way to do this is by holding the end of the 6 pieces of cord and threading them through the ring together instead of one by one. There should be roughly equal lengths of cord either side of the ring.
2. Take 1 piece of the 2 mm wide jute and make a gathering knot of approximately 3 cm long. **(Fig. 1.)**

3. Divide the 12 pieces of cord into 3 groups of 4. Take the first group of 4 cords and make 5 square knots. Repeat this with the other 2 groups. **(Fig. 2.)**
4. Take the outermost cords and pass them between the inner cords allowing you to work with the inner cords which are now on the outside, leaving a gap of 10 cm. This is done to avoid working with the same cords throughout and prevent you from running out of

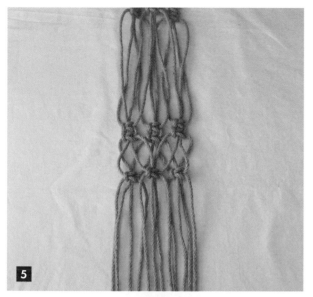

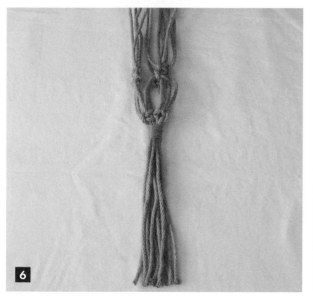

cord before finishing your piece.

5. Make 2 square knots followed by 10 spiral knots and finish with another 2 square knots. Repeat this in the 3 groups. **(Fig. 3.)**

6. Leaving a 20 cm gap, take the 2 right hand cords of any group and the 2 left hand cords of the group to the right of this one. Using these 4 cords, make 2 square knots. Continuing to work to your right,

repeat this process 2 more times so all the cords are connected. **(Fig. 4.)**

7. Leaving an 8 cm gap, repeat step 6. This time you will only make 1 square knot. **(Fig. 5.)**

8. Take the other piece of thin jute and make a gathering knot of approximately 3 cm long. **(Fig. 6.)** Trim the tail of the plant hanger to the length of your choice. I trimmed this one at 25 cm long. **(Fig. 7.)**

velvet plant hanger

This is a simple and delicate plant hanger that will look stunning in any room. Sometimes you might like your plant to take the spotlight without compromising on design. This is exactly what you will achieve with this plant hanger. I used velvet to give it a luxurious look.

You will need
- 27 m of 3 ply recycled cotton rope (3 mm diameter)
- 1 m cotton velvet (4.5 mm diameter)
- 5 cm wooden ring
- Tape measure
- Scissors
- Hook

Knots that you will use
- Gathering knot (Page 17)
- Diagonal Double half hitch knot (Page 12) Diamond Pattern (Page 13)
- Berry knot (Page 14)

Variations
Use a different velvet colour or fabric altogether or, in Step 4 instead of making a berry knot, add a tassel. If, on the other hand, you would like to tone this design down, you can leave the diamond centre empty without using any filler knots.

Preparation
Cut: 9 pieces of 3 m long of the 3 ply cotton rope and 2 pieces of 0.5 m long of the velvet fabric

AMAIA'S TIPS
- Generally, when using 1 or 3 ply recycled cotton rope, make sure that you use enough pressure when making the knots, so they look beautifully defined.
- For this plant hanger, I worked horizontally on top of a table as I found it easier to make the diamonds this way. If you would like to work this way too, fix the rope to the table using washi tape just above the start of the diamond pattern. It will not only be easier, but you will also manage to make this plant hanger a bit faster.
- Before Step 6, make sure that each group is sitting straight and unravelled as this cord tends to twist a little whilst you work with it.

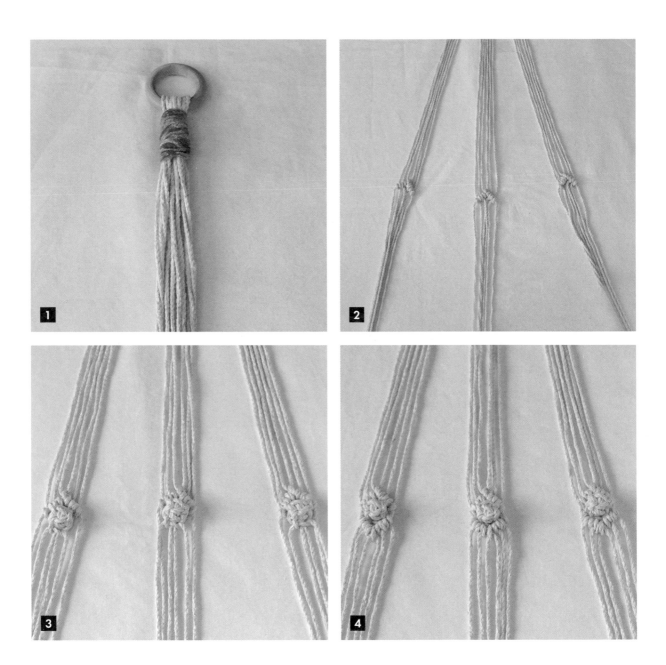

1. Hang the wooden ring in a hook. Thread the 9 pieces of cotton cord through the wooden ring. The easiest way to do this is by holding the end of the 9 pieces of cord and threading them through the ring together instead of one by one. There should be equal lengths of cord on either side of the ring.

2. Take 1 piece of the velvet and make a gathering knot of approximately 3 cm long. (Fig. 1.)

3. Take the plant hanger out of the hook and place it onto a flat surface; a table will do. Divide the 18 pieces of cord into 3 groups of 6. Tape the first group of 6 cords to the table so it is easier to work with. Leaving a 60 cm gap, take the first group of 6 cords and make a diagonal right and left double half hitch

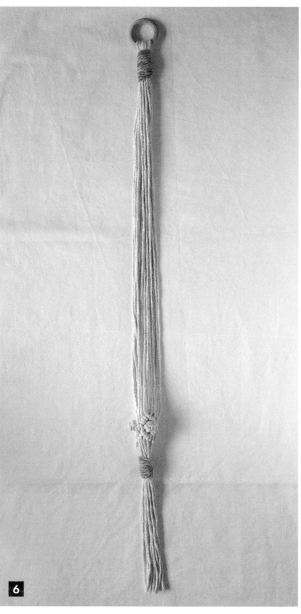

knot to create the top half of a diamond. Repeat this in the other 2 groups. **(Fig. 2.)**

4. Using the cords 2-5, make a sinnet of 3 square knots to create a berry knot. Repeat in the other 2 groups. **(Fig. 3.)**

5. Now you are ready to finish the bottom half of your diamond. Work a right and left diagonal double

half hitch knot to finish the diamond. **(Fig. 4.)**

6. Leaving 5 cm, take the last piece of velvet and make a gathering knot of approximately 3 cm long. **(Fig. 5.)**

7. Cut the tail at the length of your choice. I decided to cut mine at 25 cm long. You are finished! **(Fig. 6.)**

square knot plant hanger

Some people find it tricky to master the square knot. This plant hanger is the ideal way of practising square knots until you get them just right. This pattern will also show you how to add a new cord into an existing cord, rather than into a dowel or a ring. This is a beautiful plant hanger worth every square knot.

You will need
- 45.2 m braided cotton (5 mm diameter)
- 5 cm wooden ring
- Tape measure
- Scissors
- Hook

Knots that you will use
- Gathering knot (Page 17)
- Square knot (Page 15)

Preparation
Cut: 8 pieces of 4 m long, 8 pieces of 1.45 m long and 2 pieces of 0.8 m long

AMAIA'S TIP
- The cord add-on technique is a great way of making more intricate designs. However, if the rope is not added at the same height in all segments, it can look a bit messy. Make it easier for yourself by measuring so the rope is added equally in the different groups.

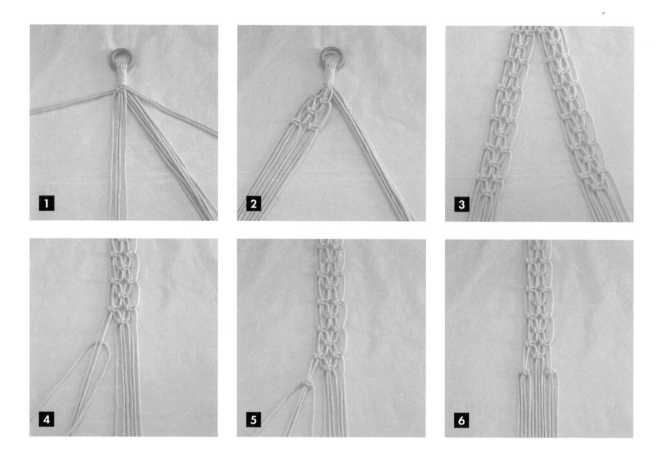

1. The first step is to thread the 8 pieces of braided cotton cord through the wooden ring. The easiest way to do this is by holding the end of the 8 pieces of cord and threading them through the ring together instead of one by one. There should be roughly equal lengths of cord on either side of their ring.

2. Hang the wooden ring in a hook and make a gathering knot of around 12 loops using one of the 0.8 m long cords.

3. Create 2 groups of 8 cords. Take the first group of 8 cords and, leaving cords 1,2,7 and 8 unused, take cords 3 to 6 to make a square knot. **(Fig. 1.)**

4. Leaving a 2 cm gap, start your alternate square knots, working 2 square knots using cords 1 to 4 and 5 to 8. **(Fig. 2.)** Leave another 2 cm and make 1 square knot using cords 3 to 6. Keep repeating these steps until you have made a set of 15 rows of alternate square knots.

5. Once you have finished your set of 15 alternate square knot rows, replicate it on the other side. Try to mimic the knots and rows you created in the first group as much as possible. **(Fig. 3.)**

6. Now it is time to start the add-on technique. Taking a 1 x 1.45 m long cord, fold it in half and place the top loop of the fold behind cords 1 and 2. **(Fig. 4.)** Make a square knot as you would normally do. **(Fig. 5.)** Add another piece of cord of 1.45 m and make a square knot with cords 7 and 8. **(Fig. 6.)**. Now make a second row of square knots right bellow these last 2. Work the first square knot with cords 3 to 6 and 7 to 10. Lastly, create a third row of square knots by only working 1 square knot using cords 5 to 8. **(Fig. 7.)**

7. You are now going to connect both groups. Leaving a 10 cm gap, make 1 square knot using the 2 right-

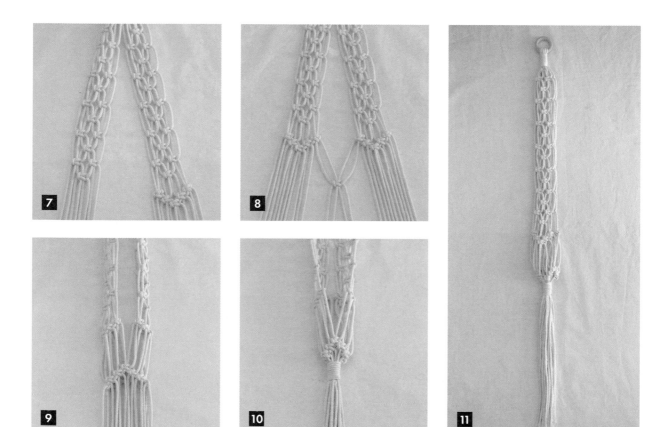

most cords of 1 group and the 2 left-most cords of the other group. **(Fig. 8.)** Repeat this step on the other side.

8. Now you are going to create alternate square knots. The 2 square knots you have just made will be the top row and the new knots you will make will come below these 2, forming an arrow. To create row number 2, use one of the top row square knots. Take the 2 right-most cords from it and the next 2 cords on its right hand side and make a square knot. Using the 2 left-most cords from this same top row square knot and the next 2 cords on its left-hand side, make another square knot. Repeat this using the other top square knot. Now make row number 3. Using the right square knot from row 2, take the 2 right-most cords from it and the next 2 cords on its right hand side, and make a square knot. Now you will use the

left square knot from row 2. Take the 2 left-most cords from it and the next 2 cords on its left hand side and make a square knot. Your row number 3 is done on one side. Repeat this on the 2 square knots left from row 2.

Connect the right square knots with the left square knots of row 3. Take one right square knot from row 3 and a left square knot from the same row that will be next to it. Use the 2 right-most cords from the right square knot and the 2 left-most cords from the left square knot and create the last square knot on this side. Repeat this step on the other side and you are almost done. **(Fig. 9.)**

9. Using the last 0.8 m long braided cord, make a gathering knot of around 10 loops just below the row 4 of square knots. **(Fig. 10.)**

10. Trim the tail to the length of your choice. **(Fig. 11.)**

double plant hanger

This double macramé plant hanger is perfect for higher ceilings or for plant lovers that are running out of space to put their plants (if that's even possible; I always manage to find a little corner here and there for a new green family addition). It's a stunning plant hanger that will make a real statement.

You will need
- 37.8 m braided cotton (5 mm diameter)
- 5 cm wooden ring
- Tape measure
- Scissors
- Hook

Knots that you will use
- Gathering knot (Page 17)
- Square knot (Page 15)

Preparation
Cut: 6 pieces of 6 m long and 3 pieces of 0.6 m long

AMAIA'S TIPS
- I recommend you make sure you have easy access to enable you to water the plants that you place in this plant hanger, especially the one in the top basket!

- As a suggestion, you can try styling this plant hanger with a filler plant in the top basket and a trailing plant in the bottom one. It makes a great contrast.

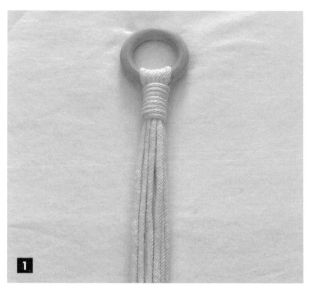

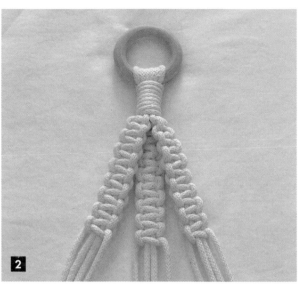

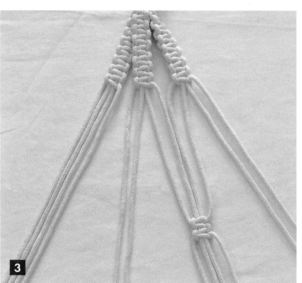

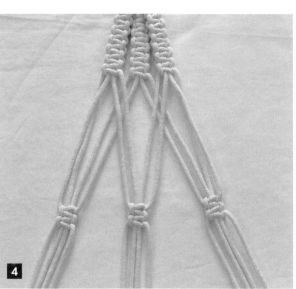

1. Hang the wooden ring in a hook and thread the 6 long pieces of cord through the ring bringing the ends together. Arrange so they lie flat on the ring.

2. Use 1 of the small cords to work a gathering knot of about 8 loops over the 12 pieces of cord. **(Fig. 1.)**

3. Divide the 12 cords into 3 groups of 4. Pick the first group of 4 and work 8 square knots. Repeat this step with the other 2 groups **(Fig. 2.)**

Turn the hoop around the hook when needed so the

cords that you are working on are facing you.

4. Start making the top basket by connecting the 3 groups together. You'll need to use 4 cords from 2 different groups. To do so, first leave a gap of 18 cm, then take the 2 right hand cords of any group and the 2 left hand cords of the group to the right of this one. Using these 4 cords, make 2 square knots. **(Fig. 3.)**

5. Continuing to work to your right, repeat this process twice more to connect all the cords **(Fig. 4.)**

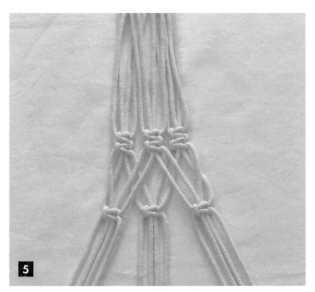

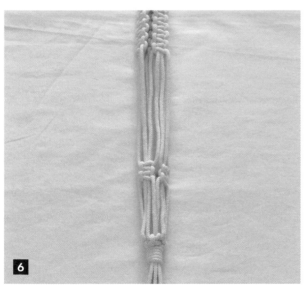

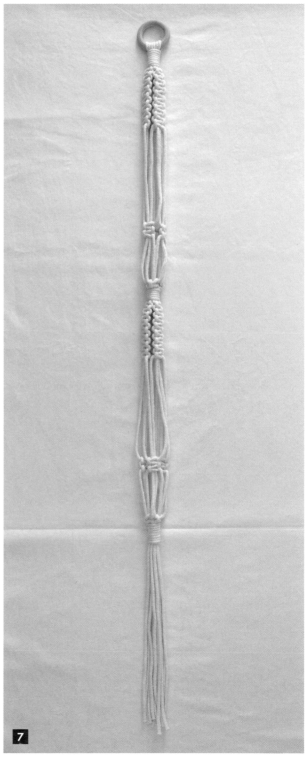

6. Leaving an 8 cm gap, repeat step 4. This time you will only make 1 square knot. **(Fig. 5.)**

7. Use the second small piece of cord to work 4 loops of gathering knots. Repeat steps 3 to 6 and using the last small piece of cord, work another 4 loops of gathering knots. **(Fig. 6.)**

Trim the tail of the plant hanger to the length of your choice. **(Fig. 7.)**

chapter two: wall hangings

Decorating empty walls at home can be very daunting. Before I hang any new wall art, I like to sketch what the wall will look like to make it easier to choose the best placement for a new piece.

In this chapter, you will be creating wall hangings in various sizes. Small wall hangings look better on smaller walls, or on a bigger wall if you are combining them with other decorative items.

Bigger wall hangings tend to be statement pieces at home. I like to hang my bigger pieces on their own, rather than combining them with other wall art or decor.

I often get asked what the best height is for a wall hanging. An interior decorator once told me to hang wall art so that the centre point of the piece is at eye level. So that's what I do.

tassels and diamonds wall hanging

Tassels are a favourite of mine. They add movement, texture and character to any piece. This design combines a set of interesting knots that create several different dimensions to this stunning wall hanging.

You will need
- 59.4 m braided cotton (5 mm diameter)
- 30 cm wooden dowel
- 2 hooks
- Tape measure
- Scissors

Knots that you will use
- Lark's head knot (Page 11)
- Square knot (Page 15)
- Diagonal double half hitch knot (Page 12)
- Rya knot (Page 18)

Preparation
Cut: 16 pieces of 3 m long, 36 pieces of 0.3 m long and 1 piece of 0.6 m

AMAIA'S TIP
- Feeling creative? I have used braided cotton for the tassels, but you can experiment using different colour braided cotton or 1 ply cotton rope instead. If you use 1 ply cotton rope for the tassels, you can always comb them so they look beautifully neat. For this, I recommend you use a groom slicker brush with thin stainless steel pins. Just make sure that the pins do not have plastic tips. Please wear a face mask when you comb your tassels as there will be many cotton particles floating around.

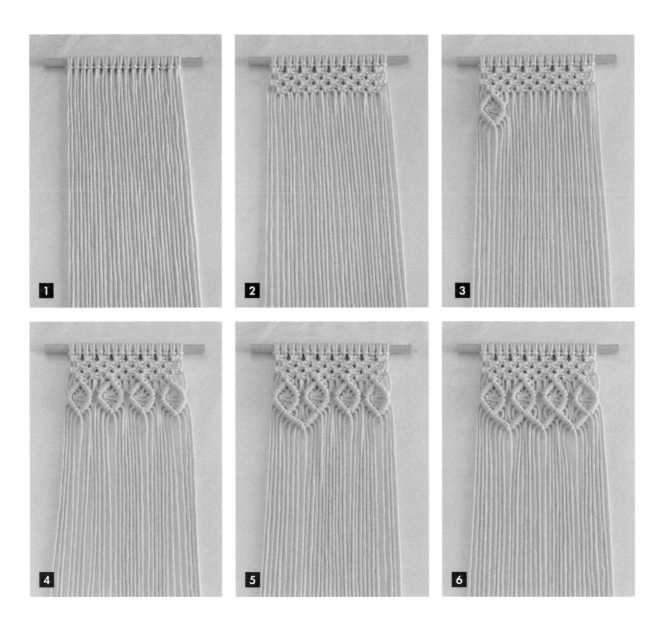

1. Mount the wooden dowel with the cotton cords working 16 lark's head knots. **(Fig. 1.)**

2. Work 4 rows of alternating square knots trying to use the same pressure for each knot. **(Fig. 2.)**

3. Work a macramé diamond pattern using cords 1 to 8 (left to right). When you have created the top of your diamond, take cords 2 and 7 to make a square knot. So far, you have only made square knots using a total of 4 cords. This time, you will use cords 2 and

7 to make it and cords 3, 4, 5 and 6 will be the filler cords. Now finish the bottom of your diamond. **(Fig. 3.)**

4. Repeat step 3 creating a row of 4 macramé diamonds in total. **(Fig. 4.)**

5 . Using cord 5 as an anchor, work a right diagonal double half hitch knot attaching working cords 6, 7 and 8 to the anchor.

Now reverse step 5. Using cord 12 as an anchor,

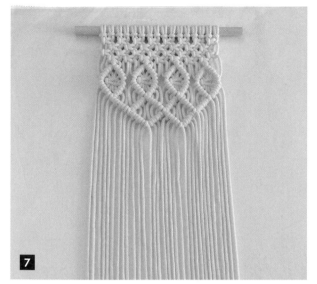

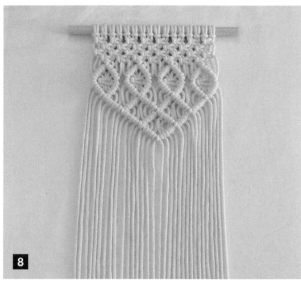

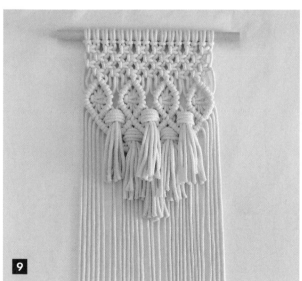

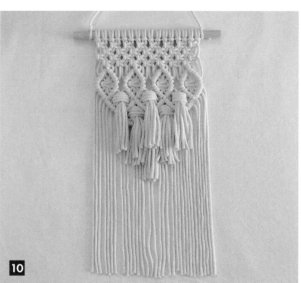

work a left diagonal double half hitch knot attaching working cords 11, 10 and 9 to the anchor.
Connect the 2 anchor cords making a double half hitch knot. **(Fig. 5.)**
6. Repeat step 5 using cords 13 to 20 and 21 to 28. **(Fig. 6.)**
7. Repeat step 5 using cords 9 to 16 and 17 to 24. **(Fig. 7.)**
8. Repeat step 5 using cords 13 to 20. **(Fig. 8.)**

9. It is time to add the tassels. Take 6 cords of 30 cm each and make a rya knot in each of the opened and closed diamonds as per the picture. Start from the bottom and work your way up. Once you have made the 6 tassels, even them out by trimming them to 10 cm. **(Fig. 9.)**
10. Take the 0.6 cm piece and attach it to the dowel as shown. You are ready to hang your creation. **(Fig. 10.)**

chunky tassels wall hanging

This wall hanging is all about chunky tassels, arrows and diamonds. Diagonal double half hitch knots are fantastic to create these designs with; if they don't look perfectly straight, don't be afraid to use your fingers to fiddle with them until you are happy with the result!

You will need:
- 63 m of braided cotton (5 mm diameter)
- 30 cm wooden dowel
- 2 hooks
- Tape measure
- Scissors

Knots that you will use
- Lark's head knot (Page 11)
- Diagonal double half hitch knot (Page 12)
- Rya knot (Page 18)

Preparation
Cut: 16 pieces of 3 m long, 36 pieces of 0.4 m long and 1 piece of 0.6 m

AMAIA'S TIPS
- Creating a diamond can be tricky if you don't apply the same pressure to all the knots. Use your fingers to delicately re-adjust your design. If you are unhappy with it, you can always undo it and start again. Practice makes perfect!

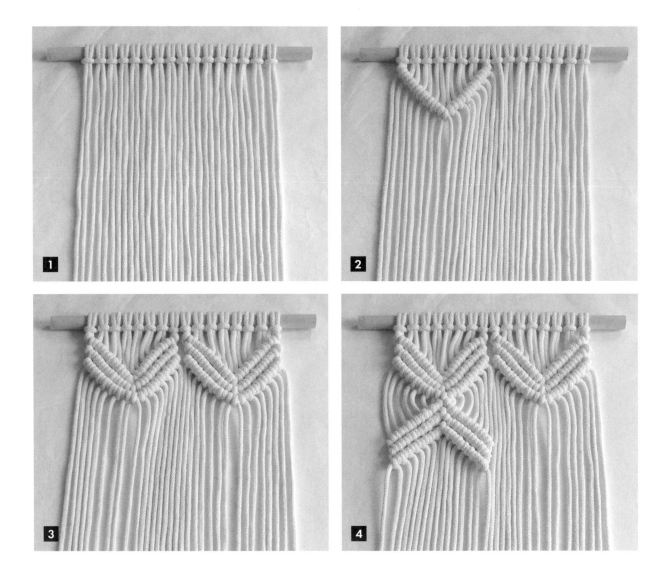

1. Mount the wooden dowel with the cotton cords working 16 lark's head knots. **(Fig. 1.)**

2. Divide the 32 working cords into 2 groups of 16. Now start working on the left group using cords 1 and 16 as anchor cords. Work a right diagonal double half hitch knot, attaching cords 2 to 8 to the anchor. Mirror this step, working a left diagonal double half hitch knot attaching cords 15 to 9 to the anchor. **(Fig. 2.)**

3. Repeat step 2 on the right group, using cords 17 to 32. Add 2 more rows of diagonal double half hitch knots in both groups. **(Fig. 3.)** For both sides to mirror perfectly, try to use the same tension in the double half hitch knots throughout the wall hanging.

4. Use cord 8 and make a left diagonal double half hitch knot all the way to cord 1. Now use cord 9 to work a right diagonal double half hitch knot. Repeat this step twice more, remembering to make a double half hitch knot on cords 8 and 9 first. **(Fig. 4.)**

5. Repeat step 4, using cords 24 and 25 as your new anchors. Then connect both patterns by making a double half hitch knot on cords 16 and 17. **(Fig. 5.)**

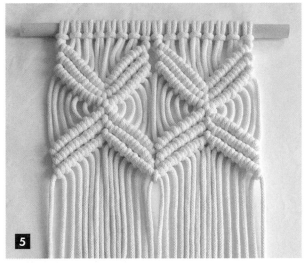

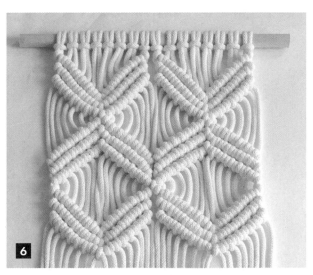

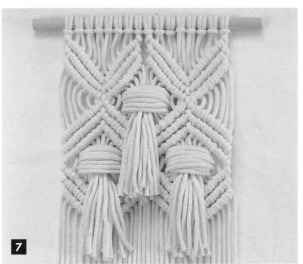

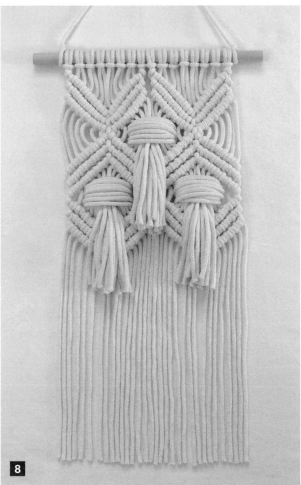

6. Now you are going to close the top half diamonds that you have created. To do so, repeat steps 2 and 3. **(Fig. 6.)**

7. Take 12 cords of 40 cm for each diamond and work a rya knot in the bottom and middle diamonds. Once done, trim the tassels to 11 cm long or, if you prefer a casual look, leave them untrimmed. **(Fig. 7.)**

8. Trim the bottom of the wall hanging to your preferred length and add the 0.6 cm cord creating a triangle so you can hang it on the wall. **(Fig. 8.)**

textured wall hanging

I really enjoy combining different knots and layering them in a harmonic way. This medium sized wall hanging is so well rounded it looks beautiful. Using braided rope makes your knots very neat, however, sometimes you just want a raw, natural and more 'imperfectly perfect' look. This is exactly what using 3 ply recycled cotton rope offers to this medium wall hanging.

You will need
- 97.4 m of 3 ply recycled cotton rope (5 mm diameter)
- 13.2 m of 1 ply recycled cotton rope (3 mm diameter)
- 30 cm wooden dowel
- 2 hooks
- Tape measure
- Scissors

Knots that you will use
- Lark's head knot (Page 11)
- Diamond pattern (Page 13)
- Diagonal double half hitch knot (Page 12)
- Spiral knot (Page 16)
- Square knot (Page 15)
- Gathering knot (Page 17)
- Rya knot (Page 18)

Preparation
- Cut: 18 pieces of 3.7 m long 3 ply cord, 30 pieces of 0.8 m long 3 ply cord, 4 pieces of 3 m long 1 ply cord and 2 pieces of 0.6 m long 1 ply cord

AMAIA'S TIPS
- If you find it difficult to work with very long pieces of rope (they tend to love to get tangled!), you can always roll the ends into a small ball to shorten them. Think small ball of yarn!

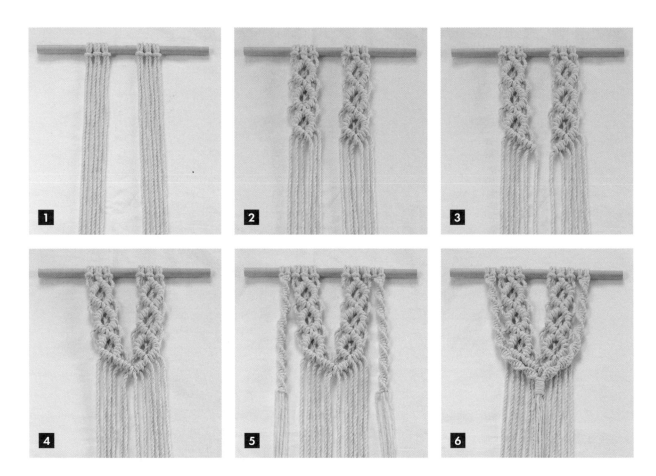

1. Start by mounting 3 x 3.7 m long cords 9 cm from the end left of the dowel, and another 3 cords 9 cm from the end right of the dowel using a lark's head knot. **(Fig. 1.)**

2. Make 3 diamonds on each side following the diamond pattern steps. **(Fig. 2.)**

3. Utilising cord 4 as your anchor cord make a right diagonal double half hitch knot using cords 5 and 6. Now work a left diagonal double half hitch knot using cord 9 as your anchor and cords 8 and 7 as your working cords. **(Fig. 3.)** Knot cords 6 and 7 together. **(Fig. 4.)** Trim all these cords to 30 cm long.

4. Mount 2 x 3 m long 1 ply cords 6 cm from the left end of the dowel and repeat this process using the other 2 x 3 m long cords, leaving 6 cm at the right end of the dowel. Work 23 cm of spiral knots

on both sides **(Fig. 5.)**. Tie them together using the 0.6 m long 1 ply cord. Work a 3 cm long gathering knot, making sure that the spirals are perfectly framing the diamonds that you made in step 2. Trim the tail below the gathering knot at 30 cm long and keep the trimmings for later. **(Fig. 6.)**

5. Get ready to work on this wall hanging's last diamonds. Mount 4 x 3.7 m long cords on the right and left hand side of the spiral knot. Using your hands, re-adjust these lark's head knots so you have 1 cm of dowel left on both sides. Work 4 diamonds on both sides. This time, you will be adding a square knot inside each of the diamonds. Once you have done the top half of each diamond, use cord 2 and 7 as your working cords to work a square knot. **(Fig. 7.)**

6. Tie them together working a right diagonal double

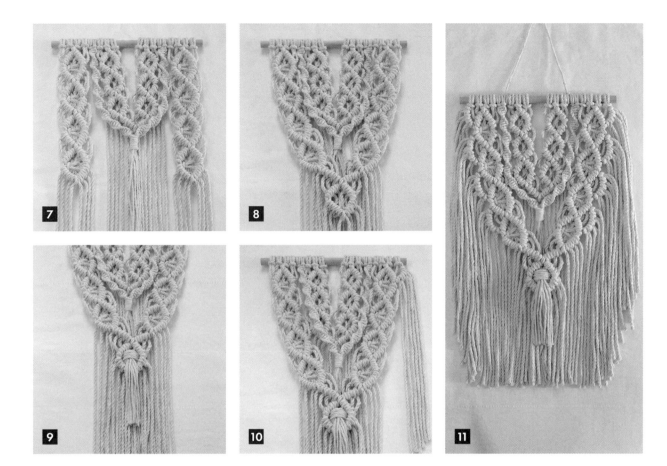

half hitch knot with cords 5-8 and a left diagonal double half hitch knot with cords 12-9. Connect the 2 leading cords using a double half hitch knot. Using these 2 leading cords, make another diamond, utilising the next 4 strands on each side **(Fig. 8.)**.

7. This step is optional. You can leave the inside of this last diamond empty. However, if you prefer to stick to the original design, you will use 4 of the x 1 ply trimmings that you set aside in step 4. Cut them in half and work a rya knot to create your tassel. Trim it to 12 cm long. If you wish, you can comb the tassel. I have left mine uncombed for a rough texture! **(Fig. 9.)** Trim all the cord that you have worked with to the same length.

8. Now it is time to finish the wall hanging by adding the side tassels. If you look at the exterior of the diamonds you have just created, you will see that they have formed loops from one diamond to the next one below - 4 in total. Attach the tassels one by one to these hoops using lark's head knots. The top right and left hoop will only need to have 3 tassels added, as they are a bit smaller than the others. The rest will have 4 each. Attach each tassel to the most external piece of cord that creates the loop. **(Fig. 10.)** Continue adding all the tassels. Now you just need to trim any piece of cord that is longer than the others.

9. Add the last 0.6 m long cord to the dowel, creating a triangle so you can hang your new piece with pride on the wall! **(Fig. 11.)**

rainbow wall hanging

During the last few years rainbows have become a symbol of hope and perseverance. I couldn't not have a macramé rainbow in this book. The earthy colours and different textures will bring warmth to any space. Rainbows lend themselves well to a nursery or children's bedroom, but would brighten any room.

You will need
- ■ 1.69 m (1.7 m to be safe) of 3 ply recycled cotton rope (14 mm diameter)
- ■ 2.95 m of taupe cotton frizz ribbon
- ■ 7.6 m of 1 ply recycled cotton rope (3 mm diameter)
- ■ 4 m of flax linen frizz ribbon
- ■ 15 cm braided rope
- ■ Tape measure
- ■ Scissors
- ■ Washi tape
- ■ Slicker brush
- ■ Large eye needle
- ■ Curved needle
- ■ Sewing thread

Preparation
Cut: 4 pieces of 35, 39, 46 and 49 cm long of the 3 ply chunky cotton rope, 1 piece 2.95 m long of taupe cotton frizz, 2 pieces of 55 cm long 1 ply recycled cotton, 1 piece of 6.5 m long 1 ply recycled cotton, 1 piece of 4 m long flax linen frizz ribbon and 1 piece of 15 cm long braided cotton rope

AMAIA'S TIPS
- ■ It is always a good idea to adjust the wrapping on the curves using your fingers, until you are happy with the look.
- ■ When you brush the end of the rainbow, especially if you are brushing it with a slicker brush, cover your mouth with a face mask. This type of brush will give your tassels a very professional and neat finish, however, it also creates a lot of fluff that can irritate your lungs.
- ■ There are endless possibilities when creating a macramé rainbow. You can add more curves, use a chunkier rope, substitute the fabrics for others of your choice or even change the colour palette. Just have fun with it! You will love the result!

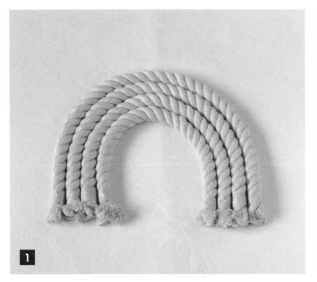

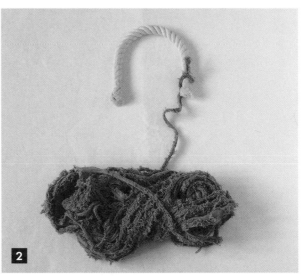

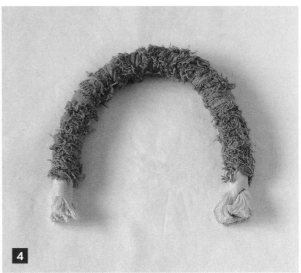

1. Lay all the pieces of chunky rope flat, forming the shape of a rainbow. Attach washi tape so the top of the tape is at 3 cm from the end of the rope. This will stop the twisted rope from unravelling whilst you work with it. **(Fig. 1.)**

2. Now let the fun begin! Take the smallest piece of chunky cotton rope so you can start attaching the yarn to it. You will start attaching the yarn just on top of the washi tape by making a normal knot. Make sure that you leave the tail of the yarn facing upwards. **(Fig. 2.)**

3. Start wrapping the cotton frizz firmly around the chunky rope until you reach the washi tape on the other end. Now, thread your cotton frizz through the large eye needle and sew a stick back through at least 2 cm of the wrapping. **(Fig. 3.)** Cut the excess cotton frizz. **(Fig. 4.)**

4. Take the 39 cm long piece of chunky rope. Attach one of the pieces of 55 cm 1 ply cotton to the rope, following the instructions in step 2. This time though,

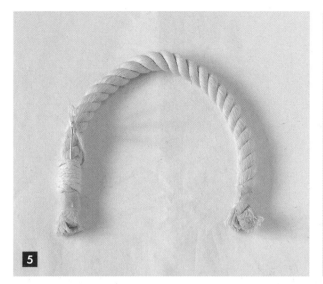

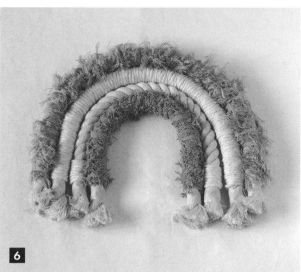

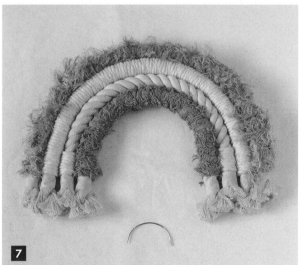

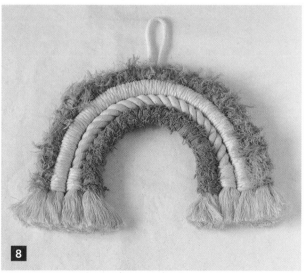

you will only wrap the 1 ply cotton rope firmly for 2.5 cm and then hide the end of the cotton behind the wrapping, helping yourself to do this with the large eye needle. **(Fig. 5.)** Repeat this step on the other end of the rainbow.

5. Repeat steps 2 and 3 on the 46 and 49 cm chunky rope using the 1 ply cotton rope and the linen frizz ribbon respectively. **(Fig. 6.)**

6. Now, using the curved needle (a normal needle will work, but will be more difficult), sew all the curves

of our rainbow together. Turn it over to work on its back and start sewing the smaller curve to the one next to it. Repeat this with the other curves. Try to use a tight tension so the curves of your rainbow are as close to each other as possible. **(Fig. 7.)**

7. To finish your rainbow, remove the washi tape and brush the ends of the chunky rope. Cut them as straight as possible. Sew the 15 cm braided rope to the back of your rainbow in a loop so you can hang it from the wall. **(Fig. 8.)**

raffia wall hanging

Raffia is such a versatile material to work with. It is made from segments of the Palmyra plant leaves. It adds natural texture and is ideal to make eye catching creations like this wall hanging. Raffia is soft, pliable, and biodegradable. It makes a great crafting medium and I love the rustic look of it.

You will need
- 150 gr of natural raffia (3 bundles of 50 gr)
- 75 cm of 2.5 mm craft aluminium wire
- Tape measure
- Scissors
- Washi tape or glue gun
- 30 cm recycled sari silk ribbon
- 2-3 clay pipe stems (optional)
- 40 cm of 2 mm jute
- A large eye knitting needle

Knots that you will use
- Reverse lark's head knot (Page 11)
- Gathering knot (Page 17)

Preparation
Cut: 48 bunches of 35 cm long raffia (allow 6-9 pieces of raffia per bunch), 1 piece of wire of around 75 cm long, 30 cm of recycled sari silk ribbon and 40 cm of jute

AMAIA'S TIPS
- Don't worry about getting exactly the number of raffia pieces per knot. Raffia thickness can vary so if the bunch that you are using for a knot looks a bit thin, add a couple of extra pieces. Because of these variations, you might end up adding more bunches of raffia if at the end it does not look as full as it should look. Play it by sight and have fun!

- Clay pipe stems can be found along the River Thames when the tide is low. I chose the ones with a bigger hole so I could thread the large eye needle without a problem.

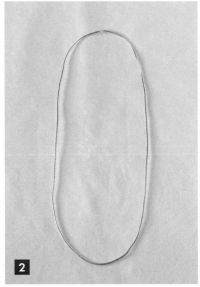

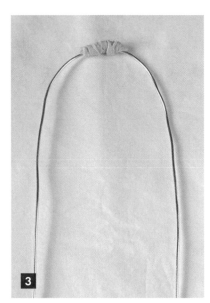

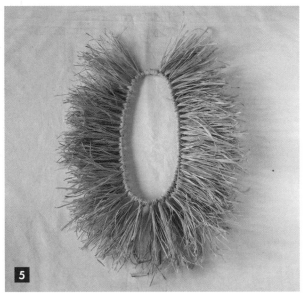

1. Using your fingers, bend the wire until you form an oval shape. It does not need to be perfect as it will keep changing shape a bit when you work on it later. **(Fig. 1.)**

2. Attach the ends together using washi tape or, if you prefer, you can use your glue gun, as I did. **(Fig. 2.)**

3. Working a gathering knot, attach the sari silk ribbon to cover the washi tape or glue. **(Fig. 3.)**

4. Start mounting the raffia by folding the 6-9 raffia thread bunches in half using a reverse lark's head knot. **(Fig. 4.)**

5. Continue adding the raffia bunches until you complete the oval. Now readjust the oval shape by gently bending the wire to your liking. **(Fig. 5.)**

6. Thread the 40 cm long jute cord in a long needle making sure that both ends are equally long. Thread

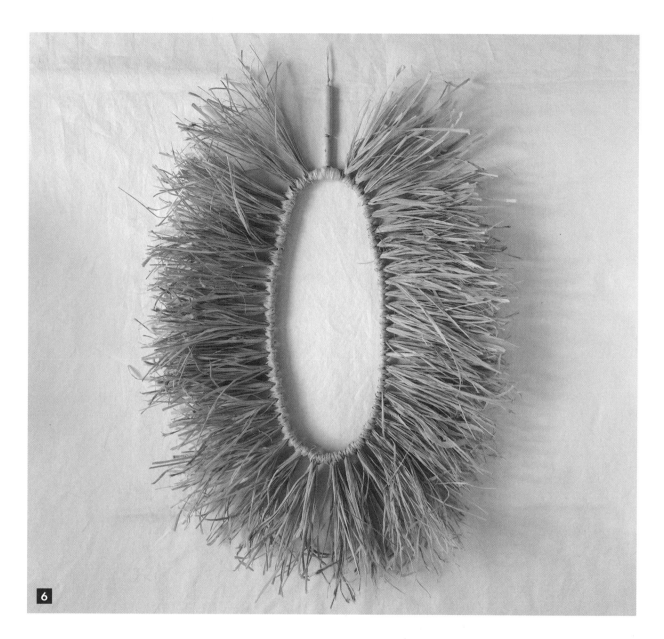

6

the jute through the clay pipe stems, if you decide to use them. Make a double knot to secure the clay pipe stems. Cut the loop at the end that still has the needle in. Now make another knot at the end of it, so you form a little loop for you to hang your new raffia wall hanging. **(Fig. 6.)**

Variations: I decided to use recycled sari silk ribbon as I had some leftover from other projects but you can use any fabric of your choice.

For a more impactful look, you can cut your raffia fibres in longer bunches than 35 cm long. Remember that if you don't like the length at the end, you can always trim the raffia fibres to your liking!

Try using banana fibre if what you are looking for is a less rigid look.

raffia leaf

This leaf is inspired by macramé cotton leaves. It is a truly original and show-stopping piece of decoration that you can hang on a wall, door knob, or decorative ladder to really give personality to your space.

You will need
- 130 cm of 6 mm jute rope
- 300 gr of natural raffia (6 bundles of 50 gr)
- Tape measure
- Scissors

Preparation
Cut: 130 cm of jute, 640 individual pieces of 45 cm long raffia

AMAIA'S TIPS
- If you want to tame the leaf a little, once you have finished, you can use a steamer to make the raffia more malleable.
- You can create this piece on a horizontal flat surface or vertically on a wall. I made it on a horizontal surface as I find it easier for this type of crafting.
- You will cut a lot of raffia so I would recommend you to do it on an easy to sweep surface and avoid any carpeted areas or rugs.

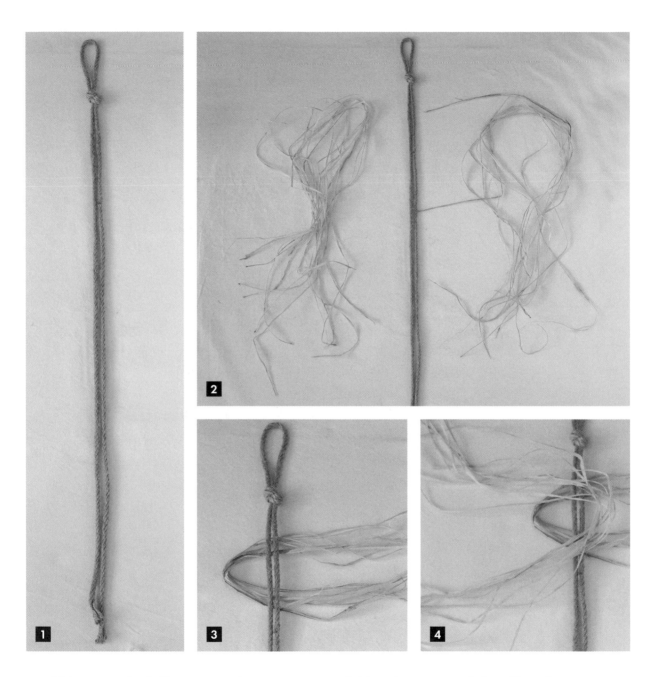

1. Fold the jute cord in half. Leaving a 10 cm gap at the top, make a loop knot. **(Fig. 1.)** This cord will act as the spine of your leaf.

2. Take 18 to 20 pieces of raffia and divide them into 2 groups of 9 or 10, depending on the thickness of each raffia fibre. **(Fig. 2.)**

3. Now it's time to attach the raffia to the centre piece. Take the first bundle of raffia and fold it in half (or as close as possible as each piece of raffia can have different lengths). Tuck it underneath the centre piece. **(Fig. 3.)** Fold the second bundle of raffia in half and place it over the centre piece. **(Fig. 4.)**

5

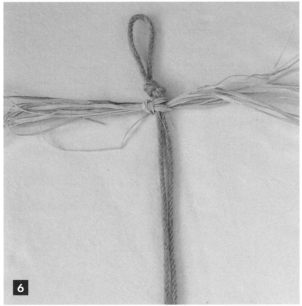

6

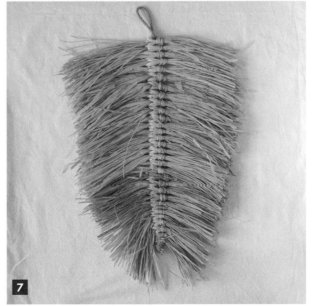

7

4. Bring the ends through the loops in both sides. Left ends will go through the left loop and right ends through the right loop. Then pull. **(Fig. 5.)** You can cut the raffia to the length of your choice or do it once you finish step 4. The raffia leaf in the project is cut at 20 cm on both sides. **(Fig. 6.)**

5. Repeat step 3 32 times. Make a loop knot at the bottom and your new leaf is ready to hang. **(Fig. 7.)**

Variations:
You can experiment by using other fibres such as banana fibre to add movement to the piece.

large wall hanging

Now that you have practised all the classic macramé knots in other projects throughout the book, it is time to create something a bit bigger!
This dynamic wall hanging will add a romantic boho touch to any room.

You will need
- 69 m of 3 ply recycled cotton rope (5 mm diameter)
- 128.5 m of 1 ply recycled cotton rope (5mm diameter) (if fringes are 50 cm long.)
- 1 m wooden dowel
- 2 hooks
- Tape measure
- Scissors

Knots that you will use
- Lark's head knot (Page 11)
- Spiral knot (Page 16)
- Square knot (Page 15)
- Diamond pattern (Page 13)
- Diagonal double half hitch knot (Page 12)
- Rya knot (Page 18)
- Gathering knot (Page 17)

Preparation
Cut: 2 pieces of 2.5 m long 3 ply cord, 2 pieces of 2 m long 3 ply cord, 32 pieces of 1.2 m long 1 ply cord, 6 pieces of 4 m long 3 ply cord, 85 pieces of 1 m long 1 ply cord, 8 pieces of 4.5 m long 3 ply cord, 14 pieces of 0.3 m long 1 ply cord, 1 piece of 0.4 m long 1 ply cord, 1 piece of 0.5 m long 1 ply cord

AMAIA'S TIP
- For a more elaborate project such as this, make sure that all the rope is cut before you start. As there are many different lengths of rope, you can organise them by putting a Post-it Note at the top of each group, noting the lengths.

1. You are going to work your way out from the middle. Firstly, mount 2 cords of 2.5 m long right in the middle of the dowel, using a lark's head knot. Then, mount 1 cord of 2 m long 12 cm away from the middle in either side. **(Fig. 1.)**

2. Take the middle cords and work 10 spiral knots. Now, link the 3 different group of cords together. Take the 2 left cords and the 2 foremost left cords from the group in the middle and, leaving a 5 cm gap, make a square knot. Repeat this step on the right-hand side with the remaining 4 cords. **(Fig. 2.)**

3. Leave a 5 cm gap and make another square knot using cords 3, 4, 5 and 6. **(Fig. 3.)**

4. Mount the 32 x 1 ply cords directly on the outer cords working a lark's head knot as follows - 12 on the top + 4 on the bottom of the left hand side cords, 12 on the top + 4 on the bottom of the right hand side cords. **(Fig. 4.)**. You have now finished the middle part of your wall hanging.

5. Going back to the dowel, leave a 3 cm gap on both sides from the middle of the wall hanging. Mount 3 pieces of the 4 m long 3 ply cord on both sides of the stick. Work a sinnet of 5 diamonds on each side. **(Fig. 5.)**

6. Connect the 2 diamond sinnets by making a right diagonal double half hitch knot, using cords 4 ,5 and 6, and a left diagonal half hitch knot using cords 9, 8 and 7. Now work a double knot using cords 6 and 7 to connect both sides. **(Fig. 6.)**.

7. Using cords 6 to 1, work a left double half hitch knot. Then, work a right double half hitch knot using cords 7 to 12. Repeat this step once more. **(Fig. 7.)**

8. Attach 24 of the 1 ply x 1 m long cords on each side of the little hoops created between the diamonds, 3 per hoop. **(Fig. 8.)**

9. You are almost there! Ready to create the outer layer? Leave a 3 cm gap from the previous work. Using a lark's head knot, mount the 8 pieces of the 4.5 m long 3 ply cord on both sides of the dowel, 4 on each side. Work 6 diamonds on each side. This time, you will fill the diamonds with 1 square knot. To do so, when you have finished the top half of your diamond, you will use cords 3 and 6 to make a square knot with cords 4 and 5 as your filler cords. **(Fig. 9.)**

10. Connect both sinnets working a double diagonal half hitch knot, as you did in step 6.

11. It is time to make a tassel to add to the middle of your wall hanging. Fold the 14 pieces of 30 cm long 1 ply cord in half and thread a 40 cm long 1 ply cord through the middle fold. Work a double knot to secure the tassel, making sure that both sides are equally long. Leaving around 2 cm from the top, use the 50 cm long 1 ply cord to make a gathering knot. Trim the bottom if not straight. Attach the tassel to where both diamond sinnets connected on step 10. **(Fig. 10.)**

12. Mount the last 60 pieces of 1 m long 1 ply cord, 30 on each side, using the same technique as you did in step 8. You will add 6 cords per hoop. Trim any of the fringes if needed. **(Fig. 11.)**

13. Attach the last 1 m long 1 ply cord to the dowel at the height of your choice and hang on the wall!

chapter three: home

When I decided to change my lifestyle to one that was more environmentally responsible, the first thing I ditched was single-use plastic. Once that was crossed off my list, I turned my attention to my home and stopped, or at least drastically reduced, buying home décor items that contained polyester, nylon or acrylic. I also tried to become a less impulsive buyer and mend or make my own clothes, decorations and accessories wherever possible.
In this chapter, you will find a collection of step-by-step projects that will hopefully inspire you to start your own journey towards making your own home décor pieces and accessories!

market bag

Ditching plastic, when possible, has been one of my top priorities for the last five years. I just love using reusable tote bags to go shopping. This market bag is perfect for picking up some groceries from your local farmer's market and also works as an everyday do-it-all tote bag!

You will need
- A clipboard or a flat surface and washi tape
- 54.8 m natural braided cotton rope (5 mm diameter)
- Tape measure
- Scissors

Knots that you will use
- Lark's head knot (Page 11)
- Square knot (Page 15)

Preparation
Cut: 2 pieces of 1 m long and 24 pieces of 2.20 m long

AMAIA'S TIPS
- I find it easier to use a clipboard for this type of project, especially for Step 3. If you don't have a clipboard, you can attach the sides of the project to a wall with masking tape.

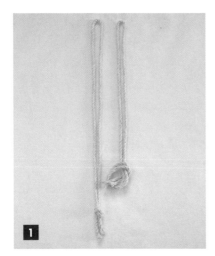
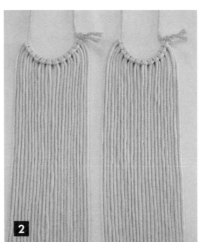

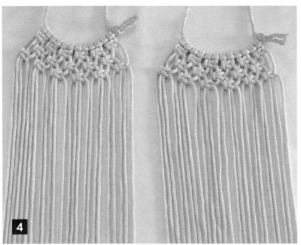
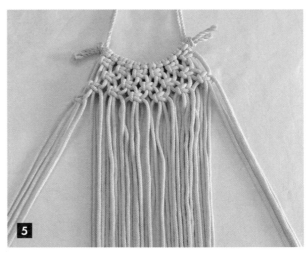

1. Take the 2 pieces of 1 m cotton cord for the handles and make a knot as shown. To do so, fold each cord in half and, using the ends of the fold, pass them under, creating a loop. Then thread them through the loop. Pull tightly, making sure that both end cords meet. Repeat this process on the other cord, checking that the knot is made at the same height as the first handle. **(Fig. 1.)**

2. Make the body of the bag by attaching the cords to the handles using lark's head knots, 12 on each side. **(Fig. 2.)**

3. To create your bag, you will make rows of alternate square knots, joining the 2 separate parts together using this same knot. Start by making a first row of square knots in both groups. **(Fig. 3.)**

4. Work a second row of alternate square knots, remembering to leave the first and last 2 cords unused. Then make a third row of square knots using all the cords this time. **(Fig. 4.)**

5. You now need to start connecting both pieces together on the fourth row. Place them one on top of the other, with the lark's head knots facing out on both sides. Leave a 1 cm gap, as you have been doing, and work a square knot using the 2 cords from the left-most of both groups. **(Fig. 5.)** Repeat on the right hand side.

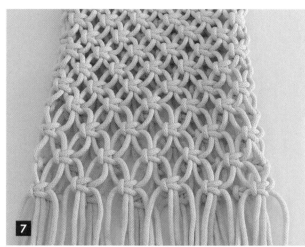

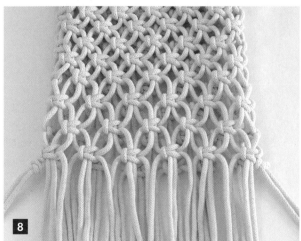

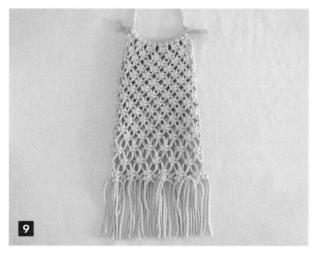

Finish the fourth row of square knots on the front and back of the bag. Try to line up the square knots at the same height on both sides. **(Fig. 6.)**

6. Continue to make alternate square knots 1 cm apart until you have made 13 rows total.

7. To give the pattern a little 'je ne sais quois', make 3 more rows of alternate square knots at 2 cm apart. **(Fig. 7.)**

8. To make the bottom of your bag, tie a knot in the same way as you made the handles, using the left-most cord from the front and the left-most cord of the back of the bag. Repeat this on the right hand side of the bag. **(Fig. 8.)**

9. To make the middle, make square knots to join the front and back of the bag and create a solid bottom. Working left to right, take the next 2 left cords from the back of the bag, and use these as your leading ropes for the square knot. The fillers are the 2 left cords from the front of the bag. Make a square knot. Repeat this process with the rest of the knots.

10. Trim the tassels to the height of your choice. I have trimmed mine to 14 cm long. **(Fig. 9.)**

Variations

For a summery look, add a long tassel, pompoms, or anything fun to one of the handles. Get creative!

tassels garland

Originally used to signify beauty and purity, garlands have been around since ancient times. They are a vibrant, almost festive way of decorating any space. This project is very versatile. You can use the garland as a wall hanging, as shown in the image opposite, display it on flat surfaces such as the top of a bed headboard or a mantelpiece, place it in a nursery or even hang it from a pergola for a special occasion. They look good in any setting.

You will need:
- A clipboard or a flat surface and washi tape
- 53.8 m 3 ply recycled cotton rope (5 mm diameter)
- 64.2 m 1 ply recycled cotton rope (3 mm diameter)
- Tape measure
- Scissors

Knots that you will use
- Reverse lark's head knot (Page 11)
- Square knot (Page 15)
- Gathering knot (Page 17)

Preparation
Cut: 40 pieces of 1.3 m 3 ply 5 mm recycled cotton rope, 1 piece of 1.8 m 3 ply 5 mm recycled cotton rope, 72 pieces of 0.8 m 1 ply 3 mm recycled cotton rope, 6 pieces of 0.4 m 1 ply 3 mm recycled cotton rope and 6 pieces of 0.7 m 1 ply 3 mm recycled cotton rope

AMAIA'S TIPS
- To make it easier to work with the long 1.8m pieces of rope, I attached them to a clipboard. I worked in sections until I finished the garland.

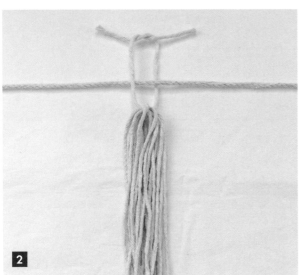

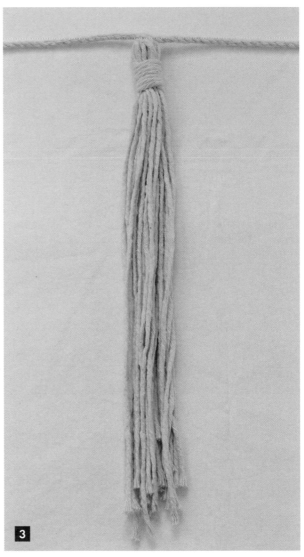

1. Start by taking 12 of the 0.8 m 1 ply cords and fold them in half to start creating a tassel. Now take one of the 40 cm 1 ply cords, thread it underneath the fold of the 12 cords and make a tight knot. **(Fig. 1.)** Attach the tassel to the 1.8 m long 3 ply cord by making another tight knot **(Fig. 2.)** leaving 55 cm from the edge.

(You will now have some excess cord, however, do not trim it off until after you have made the gathering knot below).

Using one of the 70 cm long 1 ply cords, make a gathering knot of approximately 3 cm long. **(Fig. 3.)** Trim and hide any excess cords under the gathering knot.

2. Right next to the tassel, mount eight 1.3 m 3 ply cords working a reverse lark's head knot.

Work the sequence of square knots below:

Line 1: 4 square knots using cords 1-16

Line 2: 3 square knots using cords 3-14

Line 3: 2 square knots using cords 5-12

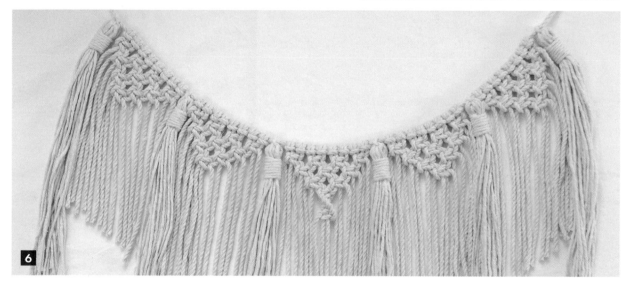

Line 4: 1 square knot using cords 7-10
Trim the ends at 20 cm long measuring from the bottom square knot. **(Fig. 4.)**
3. Repeat step 1.
4. Repeat step 2.
5. Repeat step 1.
6. For the central inverted triangle, you will repeat step 2, but on line 4 you will work 5 spiral knots instead of 1 square knot. **(Fig. 5.)**
7. Repeat steps 1 and 2 alternatively until you have a

total of 6 tassels and 5 inverted triangles. **(Fig. 6.)**

Variations
If you have colourful fibres at home, why not make colourful tassels instead of natural ones? You can use earthy, pastel or bright colours for each tassel. If you are looking for a more subtle look, you can mix natural colours with 1 or 2 other soft colours.
The possibilities are endless!

table runner

This macramé table runner won't do the traditional job of protecting your tablecloth from getting dirty, due to its loose weave. However, it will make an attractive addition to your table setting. It looks wonderful on a rustic wooden table or on top of a dark washed-linen tablecloth (as shown in the image opposite), where it adds dramatic contrast.

You will need
- A dowel of at least 3 cm diameter as this will determine the length of the fringes
- 150.80 m natural braided cotton rope (5 mm diameter)
- Tape measure
- Scissors
- Large eye knitting needle

Knots that you will use
- Lark's head knot (Page 11)
- Horizontal double half hitch knot (Page 14)
- Berry knot (Page 14)
- Square knot (Page 15)

Preparation
- Cut: 20 pieces of 7.5 m long and 2 pieces of 40 cm long

AMAIA'S TIP
- For the horizontal double half hitch knot, use your fingers to make sure that the knots are as tight and close to one another as possible. This stops the design becoming wonky. For the square knots, try to use the same pressure when making each knot, so the pattern looks as even as possible.

- You can make this project on a flat surface or a vertical setting. If you choose to make it on a vertical setting, you will need to start standing up and finish by sitting on the floor. It is always easier to fix your work to the table or wall you are working on with some washi/masking tape.

- Use the excess rope left from this project for other creations!

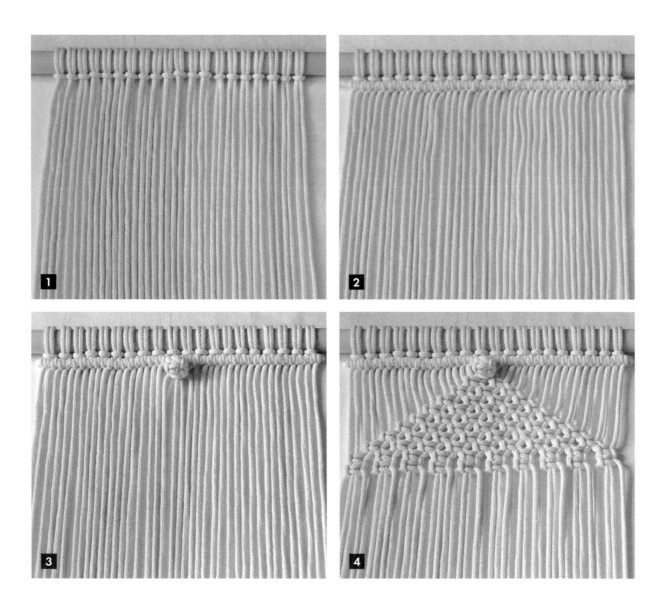

1. To start, mount the 20 long cords to the dowel using a lark's head knot. **(Fig. 1.)**

2. Take 1 of the 40 cm long cords and mount the 40 working cords to it using a horizontal double half hitch knot. **(Fig. 2.)**

3. For line 1, using cords 19-22 work a berry knot. **(Fig. 3.)**

4. Now follow the pattern to create a pyramid shape, always subtracting 2 cords on the left hand side and adding 2 cords on the right hand side as detailed

below. **(Fig. 4.)**

Line 2: Work 2 square knots using cords 17-24
Line 3: Work 3 square knots using cords 15-26
Line 4: Work 4 square knots using cords 13-28
Line 5: Work 5 square knots using cords 11-30
Line 6: Work 6 square knots using cords 9-32
Line 7: Work 7 square knots using cords 7-34
Line 8: Work 8 square knots using cords 5-36
Line 9: Work 9 square knots using cords 3-38
Line 10: Work 10 square knots using cords 1-40

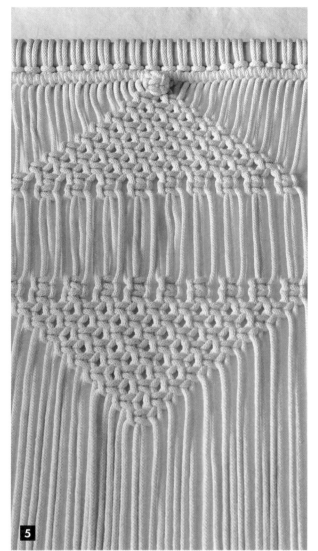

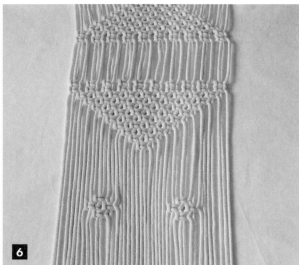

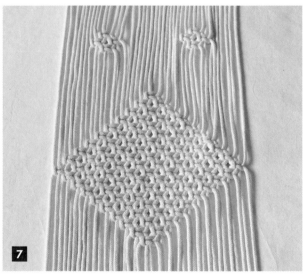

Line 11: Repeat line 10 and work 10 square knots using cords 1-40

5. Leaving a 10 cm gap, repeat step 4 in reverse order, starting from line 11 to line 1. This time, in line 1, make a square knot instead of a berry knot. **(Fig. 5.)**

6. From the bottom of the last square knot, leave a 10 cm gap and using cords 9-12, make a square knot. Now, make another 2 square knots directly below it, using cords 7-14. Finish this mini diamond pattern, making 1 square knot with cords 9-12. Repeat this

step on the right hand side of your table runner, using cords 29-32 (1 square knot) for the 1st line, 27-34 (2 square knots) for the 2nd line and 29-32 (1 square knot) again for the 3rd and last line. **(Fig. 6.)**

7. Now you will create the middle of the table runner, which is a big square knot diamond. **(Fig. 7.)**

Leaving a 10 cm gap, follow the instructions below to create your pattern:

Line 1: Work 1 square knot using cords 19-22

Line 2: Work 2 square knots using cords 17-24

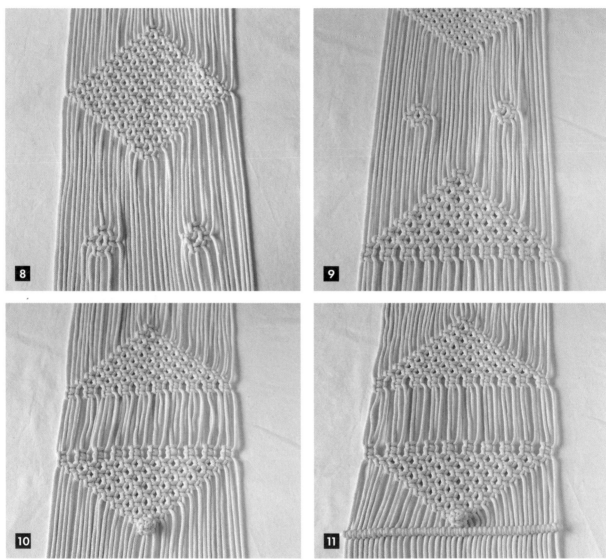

Line 3: Work 3 square knots using cords 15-26

Line 4: Work 4 square knots using cords 13-28

Line 5: Work 5 square knots using cords 11-30

Line 6: Work 6 square knots using cords 9-32

Line 7: Work 7 square knots using cords 7-34

Line 8: Work 8 square knots using cords 5-36

Line 9: Work 9 square knots using cords 3-38

Line 10: Work 10 square knots using cords 1-40

Line 11: Work 9 square knots using cords 3-38

Line 12: Work 8 square knots using cords 5-36

Line 13: Work 7 square knots using cords 7-34

Line 14: Work 6 square knots using cords 9-32

Line 15: Work 5 square knots using cords 11-30

Line 16: Work 4 square knots using cords 13-28

Line 17: Work 3 square knots using cords 15-26

Line 18: Work 2 square knots using cords 17-24

Line 19: Work 1 square knot using cords 19-22

8. Repeat step 6. **(Fig. 8.)**

9. Leaving another 10 cm from the bottom square knot you made for step 8, you will repeat steps 3 and

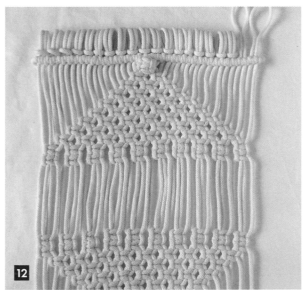

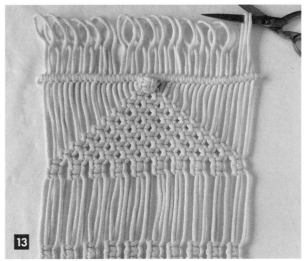

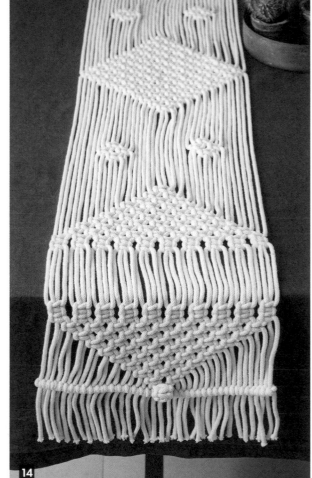

4 creating 11 new lines. However, this time don't start the top of your triangle by making a berry knot, instead make a plain square knot. **(Fig. 9.)**

10. Leave a 10 cm gap and repeat steps 4 and 3 in reverse order. Starting from line 11 all the way to line 1. This time, you will finish your inverted triangle by making a berry knot as stated on step 3. **(Fig. 10.)**

11. Leave a 11.5 cm gap from cord 1. Taking the second 40 cm long cord, mount the 40 working cords to it using a horizontal double half hitch knot. **(Fig. 11.)**

12. Remove the dowel, unravel the double half hitch knot as per **(Fig. 12.)** and create the fringe by cutting the top of the hoops. **(Fig. 13.)**

13. Trim the bottom fringe to the same length (10 cm approx) as the top. Use a large eye knitting needle to thread the ends of the horizontal half hitch knots behind the table runner and you are done! **(Fig. 14.)**

mirror

Mirrors are a great way of bouncing light around a room, especially if you hang them opposite windows or near a lamp. I love mirrors in small spaces to make the room look bigger. Make a statement decorating your hallway, master bedroom or nursery with this pretty textured macramé mirror.

You will need
- ■ A 20 cm diameter hoop. It can be any material you like. I chose copper for this project
- ■ A 23 cm round mirror
- ■ 60.25 m of 1 ply recycled cotton rope (3 mm diameter)
- ■ Tape measure
- ■ Scissors
- ■ Glue gun and hot glue
- ■ Macramé slicker brush

Knots that you will use
- ■ Lark's head knot (Page 11)
- ■ Square knot (Page 15)
- ■ Diagonal double half hitch knot (Page 12)

Preparation
Cut: 48 pieces of 75 cm long, 32 pieces of 40 cm long and 1 piece of 25 cm long

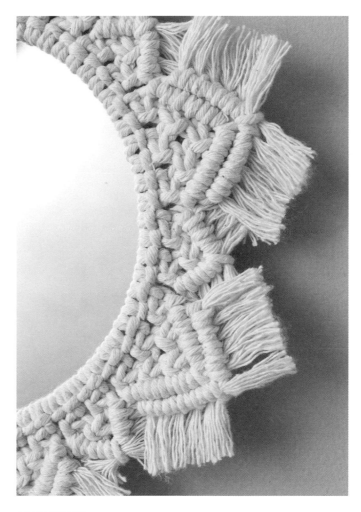

AMAIA'S TIP
- ■ If you are as concerned about the environmental impact of hot glue as I am, you can use EVA hot glue sticks. They are, unfortunately, still plastic based but they are supposed to break down more easily than other synthetic materials.

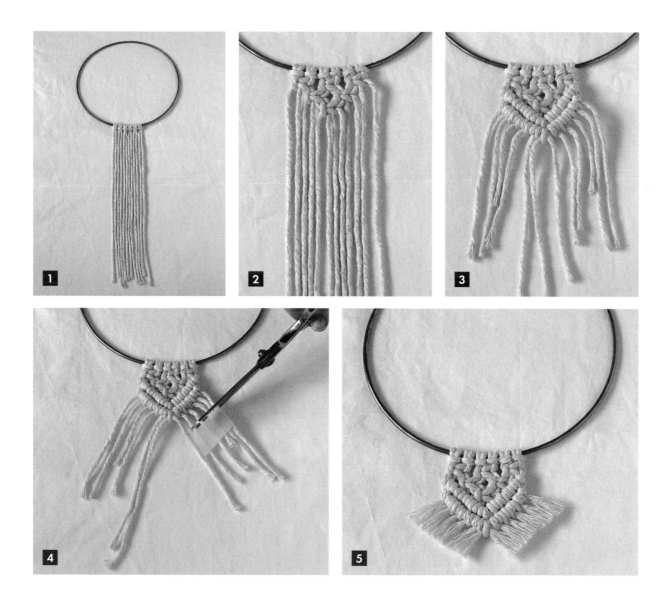

1. Mount the first 6 x 75 cm long cords to the hoop working a lark's head knot. **(Fig. 1.)**

2. Create a row of 3 square knots, using cords 1-4, 5-8 and 9-12. Create a second row of 2 square knots, using cords 3-6 and 7-10. The pattern will start looking like an inverted triangle. Lastly, for the third row, work a square knot using cords 5-8. **(Fig. 2.)**

3. Frame this inverted triangle by making two diagonal double half hitch knots on both sides. **(Fig. 3.)**

4. Cut a 2.5 cm long fringe. Help yourself with some tape to cut it as straight as possible. **(Fig. 4.)**

5. Get your face mask ready! It is time to brush the fringe. Put your face mask on and take your brush. Brush the fringe until each individual string is unravelled. As you are brushing cotton, some cotton fluff will form at the end of your fringe. Cut it once you are finished for a neater look. **(Fig. 5.)**

6. You are now going to make a smaller reversed triangle. To do this, mount 4x 40 cm long cord into

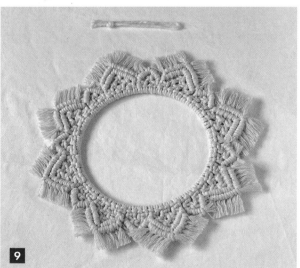

your hoop using a lark's head knot, next to the inverted triangle that you have just made. **(Fig. 6.)**

7. Create a row of square knots, using cords 1-4 and 5-8. Create a second row of 1 square knot, using cords 3-6. Frame your small, inverted triangle by making two diagonal double half hitch knots on both sides. Repeat steps 5 and 6 until you fill up the hoop. **(Fig. 7.)** If the neighbouring inverted triangle gets in the way, fold it up **(Fig. 8.)** and place it back down when you finish.

8. Take a 30 cm long cord, fold it in half and make a very tight double knot at the end of it. **(Fig. 9.)** Thread this piece of cord and mount it to the hoop, working a lark's head knot. I attached this piece between the 2 square knots of one of the small triangles.

9. Using a glue gun, place a layer of glue on the back of the macramé piece (the inside edge of the rim is a good place) and stick to your mirror using firm pressure for 10-15 seconds to ensure the mirror adheres well. **(Fig. 10.)**

dream catcher

Dream catchers have fascinated me since I was a child. The idea of a woven web that will catch bad dreams and let peaceful ones pass through captivated me. I wanted to pay a little tribute by creating my version of a dream catcher in macramé. It is a great opportunity to work with macramé feathers too!

You will need
- 25 cm wooden hoop
- 31.35 m of 1 ply recycled cotton (5 mm diameter)
- Tape measure
- Scissors
- Slicker brush
- Face mask

Knots that you will use
- Lark's head knot (Page 11)

Preparation
Cut: 5 pieces of 60 cm long, 140 pieces of 20 cm long, 1 piece of 35 cm long

AMAIA'S TIP
- I used 20 cm long pieces to make the feathers easier to create. However, you can cut the pieces for the feathers a bit shorter if you have made macramé feathers before. Cut 140 pieces of cord at 15 cm of length instead.

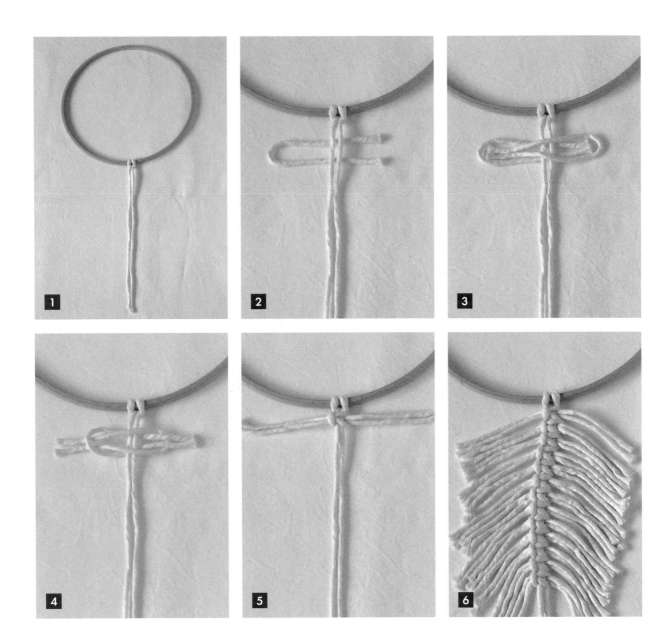

1. Fold 1 piece of 60 cm long cotton cord in half and attach it to the wooden hoop using a reverse lark's head knot. **(Fig. 1.)**

2. Put 28 pieces of the 20 cm long cord aside to mount into the feather stem that you have just created. Fold 1 piece in half. Tuck it underneath the centre piece. **(Fig. 2.)** Fold in half the second piece of cotton rope and place it over the centre piece. **(Fig. 3.)**

Bring the ends through the loops in both sides **(Fig. 4.)** and pull. **(Fig. 5.)** Repeat this step until you run out of rope and have made 14 knots. **(Fig. 6.)**

3. Repeat steps 1 and 2 four more times until you have a total of 5 feathers. **(Fig. 7.)**

4. Put your face mask on to brush your feathers. Brush each feather individually, by moving each one away from the others using your fingers. **(Fig. 8.)**

Brush the cotton away until smooth. **(Fig. 9.)** Repeat this on the other feathers. Remember to move them around if you need space to brush each of them properly.

5. Time to trim them. These feathers are 7 cm long. Readjust the feathers placing them 5 cm apart. **(Fig. 10.)** Take the 35 cm long piece of 1 ply cotton rope and mount it on the top of the wooden hoop using a lark's head knot. Tie a knot at the end to hang your dream catcher.

Variations
If you prefer a more colourful dream catcher, use different coloured rope or even dye your own cotton using natural dyes.

macramé rectangle cushion cover

Cushions are a brilliant and easy way to give a face-lift to sofas, chairs and beds. Macramé knots will help you add amazing textures and designs to make your cushions uniquely yours and give your home modern bohemian style

You will need
- 20.2 m natural braided cotton rope (5 mm diameter)
- Large eye knitting needle
- Warp thread
- Tape measure
- Scissors
- Pins
- A cushion cover measuring 30 x 50 cm

Knots that you will use
- Square knot (Page 15)

Preparation
Cut: 2 pieces of 1.75 m long, 2 pieces of 2.50 m long, 2 pieces of 3.25 m long, 4 pieces of 35 cm long, 4 pieces of 45 cm long and 4 pieces of 50 cm long

AMAIA'S TIPS
- I find it easier to work in a horizontal position for this pattern. Help yourself with some pins to fix the filler cord in place so you can use the working cord easily.

- Depending on the pressure that you use to create the different rainbows, there might be a slight difference in size in your square knots. Before you sew them to the cushion cover, use your fingers to resize them. Hold the filler cords and adjust the square knots, pulling them closer together or further apart as required.

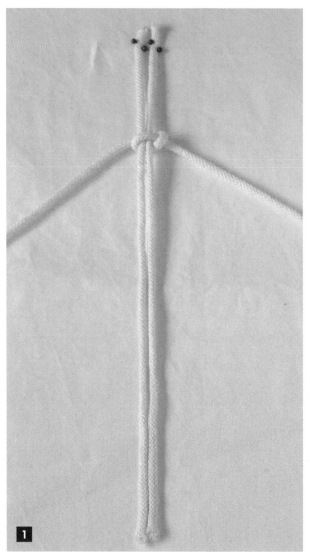

1. Start by making a sinnet of 14 square knots. To do this, take the 2 filler cords of 35 cm long and fix them to a horizontal surface (it can be a cushion) using some pins. Now take the 1.75 m long cord and fold it in half. Place the loop that this fold has created behind the filler cords, at 9 cm from the top edge. Now you have 4 cords 1-4. Make a half square knot using cords 1 and 4. **(Fig. 1.)**

2. Keep making square knots until you reach 14 complete ones. Then turn your sinnet over. Hide cords 1 and 4 behind your square knots. Using the large eye knitting needle, take one of the cords and thread it underneath the middle cords of the square knots. Do the same with the other cord. **(Fig. 2.)** Trim the excess cord. Now make sure that the top and bottom fringes (the filler cords) measure 9 cm top and bottom. Trim accordingly if needed. **(Fig. 3.)**

3. Repeat step 1 and 2 to create another sinnet of square knots of the same size.

4. Now take the 2 x 45 cm long filler cords and,

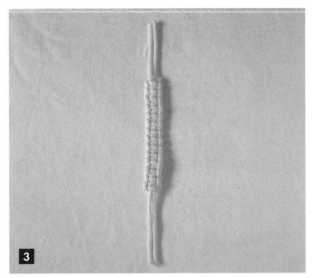

3

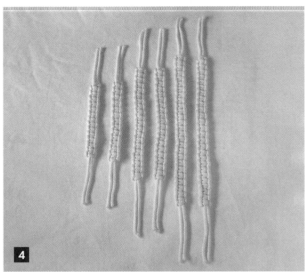

4

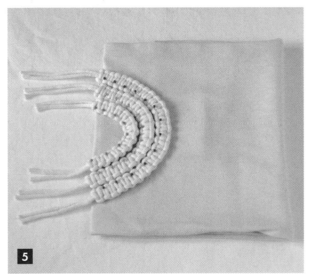

5

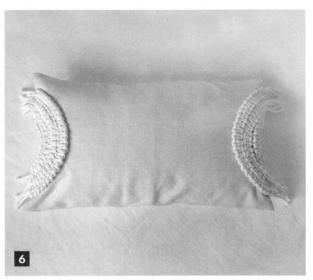

6

using the 2.5 m long cord, create a sinnet of 20 square knots. Use the same techniques as in steps 1 and 2. You will need a total of 2.

5. Finally, take the 2 x 50 cm long filler cords and, using the 3.25 m long cord, create a sinnet of 27 square knots. Use the same techniques as in steps 1 and 2. You will need a total of 2. **(Fig. 4.)**

6. Fix a small, medium and large sinnet of square knots to each side of the cushion using some pins. **(Fig. 5.)**

7. Using some warp thread, sew them in place and your cushion is done. **(Fig. 6.)**

Variations

For a warmer look, use 3 different earthy tones to create your rainbows. You can also create contrast by using a terracotta or burnt orange cushion cover, leaving the rainbows in their natural off-white colour.

macramé square cushion cover

This cushion cover design is more intricate than the previous one and is ideal if you fancy a little challenge! This design is all about texture and fringes to add a bit of movement and a romantic touch to your home.

You will need
- A dowel of at least 3 cm diameter, as this will determine the length of the fringes
- A cushion cover measuring 40 x 40 cm
- 107.7 m natural braided cotton rope (5 mm diameter)
- Washi tape (or masking tape)
- Large eye knitting needle
- Warp thread
- Tape measure
- Scissors

Knots that you will use
- Lark's head knot (Page 11)
- Horizontal double half hitch knot (Page 14)
- Square knot (Page 15)
- Diagonal double half hitch knot (Page 12)

Preparation
Cut: 26 pieces of 4 m long, 2 pieces of 1.30 m long and 2 pieces of 0.55 m long

AMAIA'S TIPS
- Generally, I find it easier to work in a vertical position for cushions like this one.

- When working on your horizontal double half hitch knots, make sure that your knots are as tight as possible. If your line of knots starts becoming wonky, adjust the lark's head knots on the dowel with your fingers, never more than the 40 cm size of your cushion cover.

- In Step 4, you can tape the end of the 0.55 cm filler cord to the wall with washi tape. This will make working on the first horizontal double half hitch knot easier. Leave around 9 cm of filler cord approx. on each side.

- If you don't want a fringed cushion, you can thread the fringe pieces through the back of the horizontal double half hitch knots using the large eye knitting needle. Afterwards, simply cut the excess rope and sew it to the cushion cover.

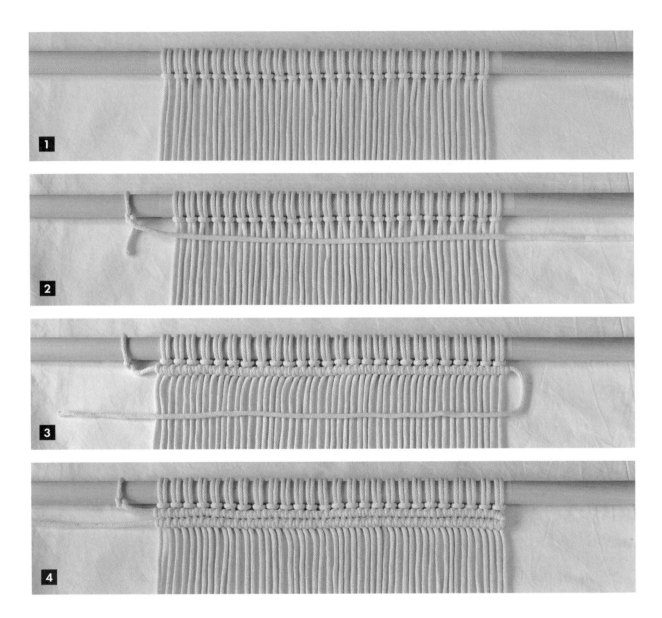

1. Mount the 26 4 m long ropes onto the dowel using lark's head knots. **(Fig. 1.)**

2. Secure one of the 1.30 m long ropes to the dowel **(Fig. 2.)** and, using it as the filler cord, work a row of horizontal double half hitch knots from left to right. Once you have made the last knot, place the rest of the filler on top of your work **(Fig. 3.)** and create another row of horizontal double half hitch knots from right to left. **(Fig. 4.)**

3. Work 3 rows of alternating square knots, leaving a 1 cm gap between rows. **(Fig. 5.)** These 3 rows should measure between 6.5 cm and 7 cm. If yours is different to this, I recommend you adjust your knots or re-do them so they equal the length of the cushion cover.

4. Using the 0.55 m long rope as the filler cord, work a row of horizontal double half hitch knots from left to right. **(Fig. 6.)**

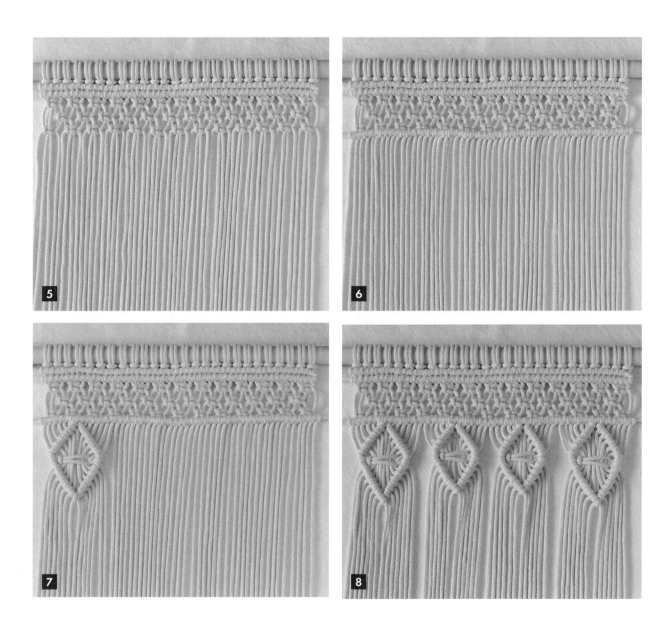

5. Now divide the remaining ropes into 4 groups of 14 – 12 – 12 – 14 ropes and create 4 diamonds using diagonal double half hitch knots.
Start by taking cord number 7 and work a left diagonal double half hitch knot, finishing at cord number 1. Now take cord 8 to work a right diagonal double half hitch knot, finishing at cord number 14. As you can see, the original cord number 7 will end up as the new cord number 1

and the original cord number 8 will become your new cord number 14.
Using rope number 2 and 13, make a loose square knot. Adjust the filler cords with your fingers if you would like them to be as flat as possible.
Work a right and left diagonal double half hitch knot to make the bottom of your diamond. To finish it, make a double knot with cords 7 and 8. **(Fig. 7.)**
6. Repeat this process making sure that you create

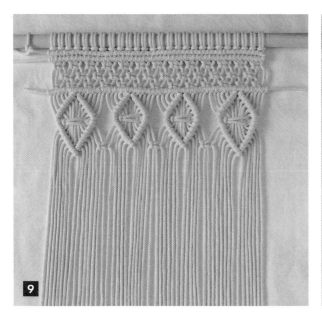

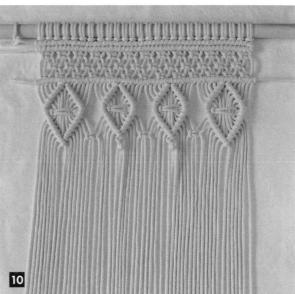

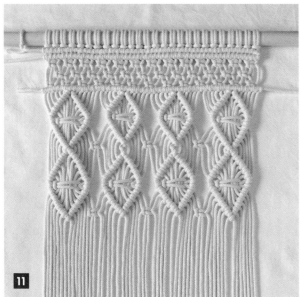

the 2 diamonds in the middle using 12 ropes each and the last diamond on the right using 14. **(Fig. 8.)**

7. Using the 2 foremost right and the 2 foremost left ropes between diamond's 1 and 2, create a square knot. Repeat this on the two gaps left. **(Fig. 9.)**

8. To adjust the height of the 2 diamonds in the middle to the side bigger ones, simply take cords number 20 & 21 and 32 & 33 and make 2 x double half hitch knots .**(Fig. 10.)**.

9. Repeat steps 5 to 7. **(Fig. 11.)**

10. Repeat step 4 **(Fig. 12.)**, step 3 and 2. **(Fig. 13.)**

11. Carefully remove your work from the dowel and lean flat on a table.

12. Unfold the lark head knots you made in step 1

and cut each rope at the centre of its lark's head knots to create your cushion fringe. **(Fig. 14.)**

13. Cut the fringes from the opposite end at approximately the same length.

14. Turn your work around and, using the large eye knitting needle, thread the tails at the end of the horizontal double half hitch knots, trimming the excess rope. **(Fig. 15.)**

15. Place your chosen 40 x 40 cm cushion cover on top of your work and, using the large eye knitting needle and some warp thread, sew the edges of your cushion cover to your macramé work. Your cushion is done! **(Fig. 16.).**

the best plants for your hangers

Indoor plants are an addiction of mine. Below you will find a list of house-plants that I think are perfect for plant hangers. It was a struggle to get the list down to my top ten!

EASY CARE
These plants are striking but easy to look after. They are drought tolerant and don't need much watering.

Burro's Tail
The Burro's Tail or Donkey's Tail is a stunning succulent from Southern Mexico and Honduras. It has beautiful blue-green trailing stems that flower in summer. It loves lots of bright indirect light.

Epipremnum Aureum 'Neon'
Also known as Neon Pothos or Devil's Ivy. Considered almost unkillable. Native to French Polynesia, this neon beauty is a joy to grow. They can tolerate low light conditions, but require bright indirect light to thrive. Avoid sunny windowsills.

Ceropegia Woodii
Subtle, delicate yet absolutely stunning, the String of Hearts was one of the first plants I bought and, with it's heart-shaped leaves, is still one of my favourites. It is native to Southwest Africa. They

like bright indirect light.

FAST GROWERS
These easy to care for plants will give your home jungle vibes!

Monstera Adansonii
One of the go tos when it comes to jungly plants, this is a low maintenance trailing plant that can also be trained to climb. Originally from Central and South America, it forms holes in its leaves which makes it a unique addition to your home. Bright indirect light is ideal for this Monstera to thrive but it can tolerate lower light conditions.

Philodendron Micans
This velvety tropical plant has pretty heart shaped green leaves with a red-purplish back. It originates in Central America and is naturally found climbing rainforest trees. It can survive in almost any light, but is happiest in bright indirect light.

The Philodendron Scandens, Heart Leaf Philodendron and Philodendron Grazielae. Tradescantia Zebrina are also lovely. The Tradescantia Zebrina, known as Silver Inch plant, has one of the most bold and beautiful leaves I have seen in low maintenance indoor plants.

This native to Southern Mexico and Guatemala has green and purple leaves with 2 distinctive zebra-like silver lines on the sides. Bright indirect light is ideal as lower light conditions result in lighter smaller leaves.

FILLER PLANTS
These will add a splash of colour and fill your plant hangers.

Stromanthe Sanguinea Triostar
Also known as Calathea Triostar, this tropical plant is native to the canopy of the Amazonian rainforest. It belongs to the Prayer Plant family, which fold their leaves up at night and unfold them in the morning. With its gorgeous green, white and pink arrow shaped leaves, this plant is all about colour. Filtered bright light is perfect but try to avoid full shade or direct sunlight.

Oxalis Triangularis
I am not a fan of purple normally, however, the Oxalis Triangularis is definitely an exception!
This plant, originally from Brazil, has beautiful and delicate butterfly-like purple leaves that open and close in response to light.
During summer, the Oxalis Triangularis can go dormant so don't think it has died and throw

resources

it away. Just stop watering it until you see new growth coming back. They enjoy plenty of bright light and can handle some morning sunlight.

Asparagus Setaceus Plumosus
Also known as lace fern, this beautiful plant is as low maintenance as ferns can get. This is because it actually does not belong to the fern family but to the lily family. It is called a fern because it looks like one. Its bushy look makes it a great filler plant for your plant hangers!
Bright indirect light is best for this plant. They can take lower lighting conditions, but direct sunlight will burn its leaves.

Tillandsia Usneoides
The Tillandsia Usneoides is the queen of air plants. Also known as Spanish Moss- although you won't find it growing in my motherland - the Tillandsia is a lush air plant that grows on tree branches in its natural habitat in Mexico, Central and South America. You can place the Spanish Moss anywhere you like as it does not have to be in a plant pot and does not require soil. It prefers bright indirect sunlight

You can find lots of of recycled cotton and sustainable materials that won't damage the environment. Here are some of my favourite brands.

RECYCLED COTTON AND OTHER FIBRES
Bobbiny
Shopbobbiny.com
Aleksandra, Tomasz and their team specialise in the manufacturing of sustainable rope in an incredible range of high-quality recycled cotton in an amazing array of colours. You will find 3 mm 1 and 3 ply cotton rope, 5 mm 1 and 3 ply cotton rope and 5 mm braided cotton rope.

Rope Source UK
Rope-source.co.uk
I get my 6 mm jute rope from here.

Rope Services UK
Ropeservicesuk.com
For the 14 mm 3 ply natural cotton rope and thicker rope, this is my go-to supplier.

Clover Creations
Clovercreationsuk.com
When in need of inspiration and unique fibres, Clover Creations is always a good place to start.

The Ivy Studio Co.
Theivystudio.co
A variety of dreamy yarns and ribbons.

GENERAL SUPPLIES
The Joyful Studio
Thejoyfulstudio.com
I got my wooden slicker brush here. They also have wooden dowels for smaller wall hangings.

G&S Specialist Timber
Toolsandtimber.co.uk
You will find longer wooden dowels in a variety of woods.

Etsy
Etsy.com
A great selection of supplies by indie businesses. Here you can find wooden hoops and hooks; airdry clay; seamstress scissors; pins; needles; etc.

PLANTS AND POTS
Cuemars
Cuemars.com
Cuemars is my number one place when it comes to buying plants and planters. They always have a great variety, including some amazing rare and variegated plants. They also source and support a wide range of sustainable local and independent brands.

about the author

Amaia Martin is a fibre artist, interior design enthusiast, environmentalist, and the founder of La Terra Macramé. Her passion for decoration has led her to collaborate with wedding planners to add a natural bohemian touch to brides and venues in the UK and her home country of Spain.

Amaia has shared her love for macramé and its mindfulness benefits through workshops in London, where she lives with her other half, Andy. Her hope is that her workshops give busy Londoners a break by exploring their creative side.

To make macramé more accessible to everybody, Amaia created DIY kits that have been sold around the world. She always supplies sustainable fibre with her kits to show the world that crafting doesn't have to damage our environment.

Amaia also shares macramé tips and inspiration on her Instagram account.

Her work can be found in a selection of independent retailers and sites across London.

Modern Macramé Style is her very first venture into the literary world.

Instagram: laterramacrame
www.laterramacrame.com

Acknowledgements Writing a book in my second language has been as challenging as it has been rewarding. Modern Macramé Style would not have been possible without Sinead from Crafty Fox Market, brand consultant, Katherine Raderecht and White Owl for giving me the opportunity to share my passion for macramé in this book. Thank you to Jesse for the beautiful photographs. I will cherish them forever. I'm eternally grateful to my amazing parents and big brother for raising me in such a supportive and creative environment. I couldn't have asked for a better family. ¡Os quiero familia! Special mention to both my grandmas, Rosalía and Dolores, and to my mamá! You have nourished my creativity and I cannot thank you enough; I learn from you every single day. Thanks to my best friends María, Janet and Robyn who have always believed in me and helped to shape the entrepreneur that I am today. Last but not least, my partner, Andy. You are my rock. You have been there for me through thick and thin. I appreciate every weekend you got up early to help me set up the gazebo for all the makers markets I attended. I love you for supporting me - from reading early drafts of this book, to living with countless bundles of rope, materials and what I call creative mess for months, if not years! And for cooking me dinner as I write these last words on a late Sunday evening. Thank you.